The Psalms
Doctor

THE SECRETS ON HOW TO USE THE BOOK OF PSALMS TO CHANGE YOUR LIFE, GUARANTEED!

Dr. Y. Bur

Available Titles

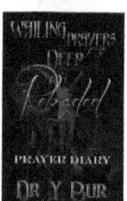

The *Psalms* Doctor

Learn the Secrets of How to Use the Book of Psalms to Change Your Life. Guaranteed!

R.O.A.R. Publishing Group
581 N. Park Ave. Ste. #725
Apopka, FL 32704
www.RoarPublishingGroup.com

Published in the United States of America
ISBN: 978-1-948936-12-5
$19.95

R.O.A.R.
PUBLISHING GROUP
www.RoarPublishingGroup.com

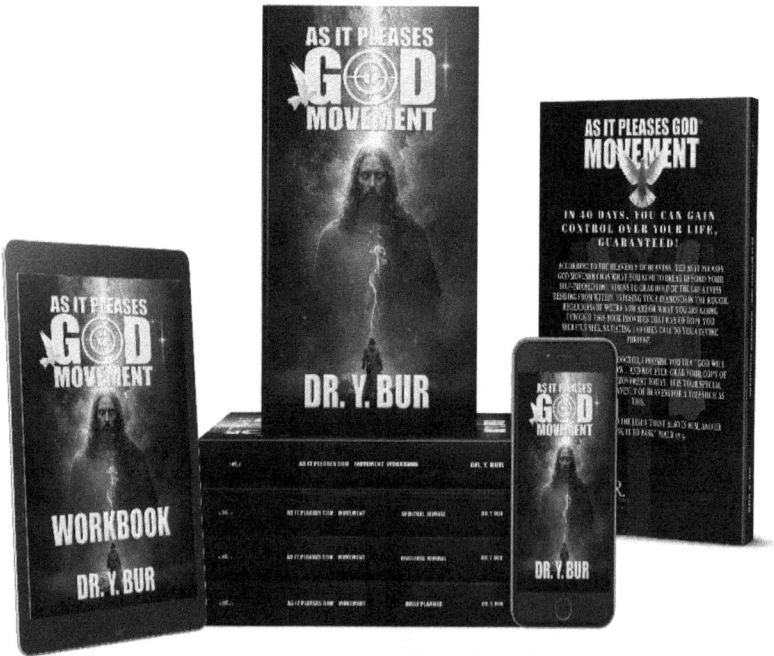

AS IT PLEASES GOD MOVEMENT

ASITPLEASESGOD.COM

TABLE OF CONTENTS

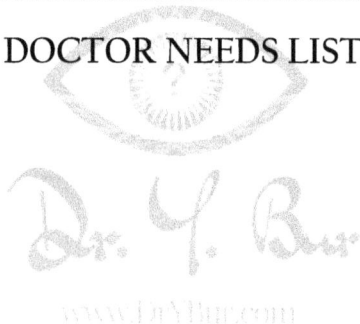

DEDICATION

As I reflect on the Spiritual Journey my life has taken, I find myself overflowing with gratitude, humility, and good theme. Through the series of winding roads, deafening obstacles, startling twists and turns, and reforming challenges, I SURVIVED. As I pen these words in black and white with my tongue becoming a pen of a ready writer, I dedicate this book to my Lord and Savior, who is first and foremost in my life. I thank Him for the love, as well as the information He has poured into the depths of my soul to ensure I can bless the lives of many. It has taken a lot of rejection, hurt, betrayal, and pain to get *The Psalms Doctor* out of me, and I pray it brings bountiful blessings in your life and the lives of others.

I want to give a great big THANK YOU to everyone who contributed to or played their role in my life leading up to *The Psalms Doctor*. Every experience has provided a valuable lesson I would not have received otherwise or would have overlooked; therefore, I am very grateful. But I would also like to give a special thank you to a very young man who OPENED my eyes to what's really taking place in the real world regarding the games people play. I was an open book for new information, I soaked it up, and now I am activating the Law of Reciprocity, giving it back to you in the Spirit of LOVE to heal the wounded and to set captives free, *As It Pleases God.*

I am so happy I did not give up on the Power of Love. Loving God, loving myself, and loving others unconditionally. And, due to my unchangeable, loving, and giving heart, God's grace and mercy gave me a promise: *"The last shall be first, and the first shall be last."*

God also spoke into my heart, saying, *"My latter days will be greater than my former days, and it will come to pass."* Amid all the hoopla and chaos, this was my promise, and it was the hope that rested in my heart with my unshakeable faith, regardless of whether I felt loved or unloved by others.

As a formal testament, the love of God and the love of myself superseded all else, regardless of how life appeared to the naked eye. Still, I was on a mission! I was on a mission to love people and build the lives of others one at a time.

Even if they did not care about me, it was my reasonable service to lead the way in LOVE regardless of how I felt. Although I appeared like a fool at times, but I accepted being mistreated and rejected like a champ. I had to learn, understand, and share the lessons behind their actions with the world. I was called to put my **SPIN** on this one thing that we take for granted, and that is LOVE. Although my perspective is a little different, it works in ways that only the human psyche will respond.

If we've had love all our lives, then we do not know what it's like to go through life being truly unloved. Therefore, we take it for granted, becoming selfish and unreasonable to those who fall out of our circle of love. Is this fair? Absolutely not!

In the Eye of God, what is fair or unfair is indeed a matter of opinion. However, if a person has not experienced what it feels like to go through life with a smile on their face, knowing the only person that's really on their side is GOD, they would think and behave differently. For this reason, I share The Psalms Doctor to ensure everyone will have an equal opportunity to love and be loved effectively.

As I present this book to the world, I ask readers to consider their role of faith in their own lives. You see, each of us has a measure of faith, and we also have our own story to tell with a unique tapestry of experiences that shape our Spiritual Journeys. Yet, we hide it from ourselves and others without truly learning the lessons hidden within it.

In The Psalms Doctor, I welcome you to put a new perspective on your faith. One that will guide, inspire, and ultimately bring you back to where you belong, and that is in the Arms of God, your Heavenly Father, and under His Divine Wing.

In fostering a deeper understanding from hopelessness to joy, anger to peace, hatefulness to love, impatience to patience, unkindness to kindness, wretchedness to goodness, unfaithfulness to faithful, abrasiveness to gentleness, and recklessness to self-control, each Psalm offers a glimpse into the depths of the human psyche and experiences that we do not often understand or talk about in real-time. While simultaneously revealing the steadfastness of God's love in the Ancient Scroll of Psalms, connecting you back to Him, Spirit to Spirit.

As I dedicate these Divine Perspectives to you, Spirit to Spirit, to avoid navigating through a dense fog and unsurety, I have placed this Divine Wisdom on a silver platter for you to glean. These Spiritual Principles and Perspectives took many battle scars to obtain, helping to guide you through your personal journey in life.

The Divine Wisdom, Understanding, and Instructions in this book, and all of my books with the *As It Pleases God®* Movement, came at a cost that I am pretty sure you would never want to pay. All of which were designed for me to leave my Spiritual Mark with a reservoir of SOUND and PROVEN information for generations to come. Therefore, use the valuable lessons, information, and perspectives wisely, and rest assured, resilience, growth, and transformation will become your portion.

As Dr. Y. Bur, The WHY Doctor, I pray that you can proactively avoid unnecessary pitfalls by learning from these stories. Feel free to use them as a beacon of hope and light for yourself and others as you navigate your path with greater clarity and purpose, *As It Pleases God.*

INTRODUCTION

Having an ITCH you cannot scratch is one of the worst feelings you could ever experience. However, when it comes down to having an ITCH from within, then what do you do? How do you coax the ITCH that will not go away? Then again, what do you do about an ITCH causing much embarrassment and losses? This book reveals the secrets of how to deal with Mental, Physical, Emotional, and Spiritual woes to ensure you get exactly what you want, need, desire, and deserve out of life, *As It Pleases God.*

Applying *The Psalms Doctor* is the best way to gain control over our lives and to learn the difference between our perception and our reality. We will always find ourselves talking about living a great life, but why do we often make it such a challenging task when it's just a choice away? Better yet, one prayer away?

If we take a moment to reflect on our past choices, we will find that it has been our perception and the lack of prayer that have caused the most problems in our lives, as opposed to the people, places, and things around us. I know about this all too well, and it's my reasonable service to share *The Psalms Doctor* with those who have a willing ear to hear about what brought me to my present state of mind.

Like many, I speak and pray to God every day; I express the desires of my heart and the lack thereof. I also give thanks in all things, the good, and the not-so-good as well. But, more importantly, I ask God every morning to allow me to become a blessing to others; therefore, He gives me wisdom, hope, and the motivation to inspire others as well as myself. My greatest gift is the ability to motivate and encourage others through whatever I'm dealing with, going through, growing through, or praying through.

I walk in my destiny every day by finding ways to encourage or spark greatness within everyone I come in contact with. Why? My mission is to enhance the lives of others one at a time, as well as to enhance my own life every single day by becoming better, stronger, and wiser with a work-in-progress mentality.

In this journey called life, I look for ways to learn something new; actually, it's like an expectation for me. I expect nothing less than learning more than I did the day before, building my repertoire of wisdom. While simultaneously discarding or recycling what I do not need. Why? I must cleanse my mind of all the unwanted things that have the potential to shift my way of thinking from positive to negative. I will also remove anything or anyone having the potential to clutter my mind with unfruitful thoughts or rotten fruit. And so should you!

You are the best doctor in your life, and if you delegate this role to someone else, then you will become slighted. Why does slighting occur? They do not have the Godly prescription for your soulish nature; you do! For the record, God will never give the psyche's prescription to another man.

It is always hidden within, even if you are gleaning from another man's repertoire.

When decluttering and cleansing my Mind, Body, Soul, and Spirit, some may think I am a little insensitive when opting out of negativity. Still, in order for the Book of Psalms to work on my behalf as a doctor in my life daily, I must follow instructions. Why? Simply put, is it not through our thoughts that actions are taken?

Am I perfect? Absolutely not! I have issues, strengths, and weaknesses like everyone else. I just make it my business to focus 80% of my time on my strengths and 20% of my time to work on my weaknesses without passing judgment. I assume total responsibility for myself, my life, my dreams, my goals, and my mishaps in life. I know exactly what I want and do not want, so it's my responsibility to get what I want and get rid of what I do not want, right?

According to the stats, most of us settle for less than what we deserve due to our impatience. We are in a right now world, and what one person will not do, another one will, right? Yes and No. Unfortunately, the 'right now' satisfaction is not always the best. For instance, the digital age has conditioned us to expect quick results with instant microwave rewards. Not realizing some things take time in the Eye of God, *As It Pleases Him.*

As I take this a step further, social media platforms, streaming services, and even fast food joints have contributed to an atmosphere where waiting is deemed as a problematic flaw, rather than a Divine Virtue. Actually, impatience often makes us look like boo boo the fool for making hasty decisions, violating our conscience, not seeing the red flags, or becoming blinded by our wants, needs, and desires. Clearly, I am not pointing the finger here...It is through experience that I am able to present this Divine Wisdom for a time such as this. The bottom line is that impatience is detrimental to our well-being and to the human psyche, causing us to settle where we do not belong or forfeit what rightly belongs to us.

When dealing with matters of the heart and mind, we need time to think, pray, listen, and understand what we are doing before we engage or commit to something or someone. Why do we need time? A rushed or uninformed decision may incorporate our deepest regrets, especially when we do not add God into our equational efforts. Then again, we can make an absolute mess in our lives, whether through poor decisions, unexpected circumstances, or a chain of events that spirals beyond our control, that it would take years to recover from.

In doing your due diligence, using the Book of Psalms can indeed help in communing with God, *Spirit to Spirit*. The strategic collection of poetic prayers and hymns not only evokes Spiritual Reflection within the psyche of mankind. But it also serves as a valuable Spiritual Tool used to guide, teach, and inspire us through the expression of authentic emotions that we often hide. At the core, Psalms capture the full spectrum of our human experiences, including the feelings of joy, sorrow, debauchery, anger, gratitude, love, and longing.

In provoking genuine dialogue in your alone time with God, *Spirit to Spirit*, as Dr. Y. Bur, The WHY Doctor, I present to you, *The Psalms Doctor,* to cultivate a life of faith, authenticity, reflection, connection, and resolve. So, when life throws you a curveball, you will know what to do, how to do it, and why you are doing so with purpose, fulfillment, passion, and growth.

CHAPTER 1

THE LOVE DOCTOR

Love is what we do. Love is who we are. Love is absolute, even if we feel deprived. *The Love Doctor* is on the scene, helping those who are willing to help themselves by moving forward in the Spirit of Excellence. How do we move forward, especially when there is a love deficit? First, we need God. Secondly, a love deficit is a perception governing our mindset. Thirdly, a shortage of love could never exist as long as we extend it with no strings attached.

By changing our mindset through doing a positive reversal of a negative thought, feeling, or desire, we can bring forth our personal *Love Doctor*, which is hidden within our very own psyche. Really? Yes, Really! Let's go deeper.

Why do we do what we do? Why do we say what we say? Why do we think the way we do? Or, better yet, why do we not love the way we should? The WHYS of life give us an opportunity to understand ourselves when we are misunderstood regarding:

- [ ] What we are or are not doing.
- [ ] What we are or are not saying.
- [ ] What we are or are not becoming.
- [ ] Who we are or are not loving.

Love and Freedom are all around us; we cannot get away from them. But the question remains: Why does love or the lack of freedom hurt so badly? Why does love or the lack of freedom deceive us? Why do love and bondage break our hearts? Why, Why, Why, Why...Can someone really answer these questions? The answer is yes. That someone is Y.O.U. Yes, this is correct; you are the only one who can honestly answer the WHY of your Version of Love and Freedom.

As *The Psalms Doctor*, not answering your soulish questions creates an ITCH from within the depths of your soul. Why? Where there is a perceived lack of love, there will always be a lack of freedom, Mentally, Physically, Emotionally, Spiritually, or Financially. Unbeknown to most, the deprivation of love is the primal seed, bringing forth roots and fruits of all the issues we face today.

By simply asking fact-finding questions of purpose, passion, and desires, we can jumpstart the Mind, Body, Soul, and Spirit. Then again, taking the time to understand the what, when, where, how, and why of love and freedom, we then get the precious privilege of opening the gate to the Fountain of Wisdom that's buried within the depths of our very own soul. Yes, we have the answers within us. All we have to do is seek the answers from within instead of getting superficial opinions from people who are not connected to our souls.

I am not implying that receiving advice is wrong. I am saying the advice we receive from someone should bring confirmation and alignment. If it is not, then we have work to do from the inside out.

When working on ourselves, oops...when doctoring on ourselves, *As It Pleases God*, we have less time to focus on being judged or judging others on what we may be guilty of ourselves. Why? Our past repertoire of secrets filed under a different label is not something we want to broadcast, bringing shame to our names. Therefore, if we mind our own business, we have less time to meddle or get our perception of our reality twisted.

The Psalms Doctor is not for the faint of heart; if you desire LOVE and FREEDOM, you must put in the work to ensure you fill in the blanks, *As It Pleases God*, getting out of your own way. Then again, if you are gung-ho on pleasing yourself, unfortunately, this book is not for you. It aims to Spiritually Align and Equip you with the knowledge, understanding, and know-how to unleash GREATNESS.

As life would have it, the Plan of God is not set in stone for anyone. Why? He did not create robots, nor will He violate your FREE WILL! Everyone is different, and everyone will have their own path in life; therefore, you have options, choices, lessons, and repercussions. Regardless of where you are or what you have going on, they will define the chapters of your life, unveiling your Divine Blueprint or burying it.

Throughout my journey, I have found that LOVE is the foundation of all things. When we lack love or become cold-hearted, we will lose our way in life by default from the inside out. Why would this happen, especially when having free will to love or not to love? We are relational beings, and the moment we remove love from our equational efforts, we leave room for hate to breed within the human psyche, similar to mold spreading.

In the same way that mold has free will to grow, whether we like it or not, when the conditions are conducive, it will grow and multiply until we do something about it. If not, it can become detrimental to our well-being, regardless of our awareness or heart posture.

The opposite of love is evil, and if you read evil backward, it tells you to LIVE! They are all connected, and if we are not exhibiting love, then what are we exhibiting? There is no in-between on this one! Whether we exhibit love or evil, they affect how we live.

In the Eye of God, one must become very cognizant of one's actions, reactions, thoughts, beliefs, words, and desires on a moment-by-moment basis. Self-control in these areas ensures the coldness of life does not create a vessel of ice, a heart of stone, a bed of waywardness, or a knucklehead of foolery.

King Solomon in the Bible put together several proverbs to guide us in practical wisdom regarding life skills to safeguard our blessings. In addition, it prevents us from cursing our own hands and brings structure to the Mind, Body, Soul, and Spirit. As his legacy lives on, the same wisdom that he asked for, is available to us. We only need to ask, follow instructions, and use them to the best of our ability, *As It Pleases God.*

The Voice of Wisdom says in Proverbs 8:1-4, *"Does not wisdom cry out, And understanding lift up her voice? She takes her stand on the top of the high hill, beside the way, where the paths meet. She cries out by the gates, at the entry of the city, at the entrance of the doors: "To you, O men, I call."* It doesn't matter how we may or may not feel about reading the Bible, but there are indeed hidden truths that ungodly individuals have mastered to outsmart Godly ones. Undoubtedly, I am not here to judge who exhibits Godly characteristics and who does not. As *The WHY Doctor*, my goal is to empower willing vessels with vital lifesaving information with Biblical Alignment, *As It Pleases God*.

Now, with this in mind, our WHY in life is directly linked to our emotions. If we do not learn how to heal or deal with our emotional self, it will definitely become hard to deal with someone else's Version of Love.

Although we all have our perception of love, there are rules, strategies, guidelines, and concepts of love we must uncover to be able to love God, love self, and love others as if one has never been hurt before. If not, we are destined to become enslaved by something or someone, creating a form of bondage within the psyche or traumatizing us to the core.

As life progresses with or without us, the wisdom and love I have put into *The Psalms Doctor* has an insurmountable treasure chest of benefits. These hidden jewels are designed to teach us the SPIRITUAL way of getting what we want without creating enemies along the way. Here are some of the learnable and jewel-like benefits available, but not limited to such:

- ☐ You will learn how to love effectively, *As It Pleases God*.
- ☐ You will learn the reverence and fear of God.
- ☐ You will learn the value of loving everyone.
- ☐ You will learn wisdom and discipline.
- ☐ You will learn the value of understanding.
- ☐ You will learn how to receive and obey instructions.
- ☐ You will learn how to deal with life lessons.

- [ ] You will learn how to value knowledge.
- [ ] You will learn how to exercise discretion.
- [ ] You will learn why we need to exercise prudence.
- [ ] You will learn how to embrace wise counsel.
- [ ] You will learn how to treat people.
- [ ] You will learn the value of respect.
- [ ] You will learn the importance of humility.
- [ ] You will learn who to hang out with or who to avoid.
- [ ] You will learn how to develop Godly character.
- [ ] You will learn how to treat your parents or your elders.
- [ ] You will learn about the rod of correction.
- [ ] You will learn how to break free of any form of bondage.

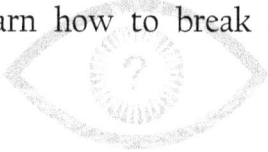

The Psalms Doctor brings the GOOD NEWS and GOOD TIDINGS of LOVE to all who are willing to receive it on a SILVER PLATTER. Now it is your time to take a moment to look within for the answers to life's most mind-boggling questions.

As your inner wisdom awaits your quest or queries to your WHY, it is not required to release it until you are ready to receive it. In a world where heroes, champions, role models, and idols are created, there are a vast amount of people who are really great, but do not realize it. The Mind, Body, Soul, and Spirit are consumed with an ITCH they haven't a clue how to scratch. As a result, they find themselves filling in the blanks while plugging and playing as they go along.

An ITCH from within is basically a longing we all have, some more than others, but we all have a longing from within for something or someone. An inner ITCH can also be referred to as an inner struggle, spiritual warfare, vexed spirit, soul tie, yoke, or longing. The difference is that some people understand that they need help and need to work on themselves every single day, and some couldn't care less about inner growth.

According to the Heavenly of Heavens, an ITCH that is not scratched or soothed, *As It Pleases God*, will become much stronger and contagious. Plus, it will cause us to settle for people, places, and things we are not happy with or temporarily fill a void, only to become an inner pit in due time.

PRAYER

I will have what I decree...I will have whatever I desire, and I will have what God has destined for me, with clean hands and a pure heart. God, You are my point of Divine Provision. I will not have any want or need in my life that contradicts Your Divine Purpose.

I know it is Your will for me to have love, prosperity, peace, purity, and greatness beyond any human imagination. Father, my God, I also know it is Your will for me to be submerged in good health, strength, sound mind, and stability without any regrets attached to it, in the Name of Jesus.

Henceforth, I declare and decree light is brought to the dark areas of my life, as Your word becomes the lamp under my feet, and a light unto my path, O' Lord, my Strength, and my Redeemer. Let this light destroy all darkness that's hovering over me, my finances, my mental state of being, my emotional stability, or any area of my life.

I take authority over, break, and destroy all negative energies or forces designed to sift me. As the deep calleth unto the deep, I invoke DIVINE protection and oneness with the Holy Spirit as You allow my Guardian Angels to clear my path of all unwanted or harmful debris, influences, or obstacles designed to sift me as wheat.

By the Spiritual Power vested within me, I will have what I decree because love is my portion. Right now, in the Mighty Name of Jesus, I decree good health, blessed wealth, a great attitude, and good success.

While my gift makes room for me, placing me before men in high places with favor beyond all human understanding, I will wait on You, my Heavenly Father. Thank you, and Amen. Amen. Amen.

SCRIPTURE READING:

PSALMS 23
PSALMS 47
PSALMS 103
PSALMS 116
PSALMS 135

CHAPTER 2

GET TO THE ROOT

Life, as we would call it, has a structural connection to everything and everyone we hold dear to us. We can call it a ROOT, Branch, or Bloodline, but in the Eye of God, they are all the same. Our past creates an element of our present struggles from within, controlling our present and future actions, reactions, attitudes, thoughts, beliefs, desires, conditioning, and demeanor. More importantly, if we do not *Get To The Root* of it, them, or that, it determines our level of greatness, ITCH from within, and the quality of fruits produced.

For example, the people with the worst attitudes are usually the ones with the biggest and most hidden ITCH. Although we have all suffered some form of known or unknown abuse, trauma, or setback, the ones with the biggest ITCH are usually the ones who are in the most denial or refuse to *Get To The Root* of whatever, whenever, or however.

A person with an ITCH from within is most often depressed or stressed all the time, with a short fuse. We will also find that their self-worth is so damaged that their self-esteem drops to an all-time low, subjecting them to abuse in many forms. Whether they are the abuser or the abusee, there are a few reasons why an individual abuses others or tolerates abuse:

- ☐ Loneliness
- ☐ Anger
- ☐ Insecurity
- ☐ Low self-esteem
- ☐ Conditioning
- ☐ Helplessness
- ☐ Broken heart
- ☐ Trauma
- ☐ Lack of love
- ☐ Grieving
- ☐ Fear
- ☐ Dependency

An unknown author once said, "Anger is one letter short of danger." To protect myself, I stay away from individuals who are angry, evil, or hateful all the time. For me, it's like a time bomb waiting to happen. Actually, most people only think of abuse as being physical; however, many different forms of abuse contribute to an irritating ITCH of an abuser and their victims. Let's talk about the different forms of abuse:

PHYSICAL ABUSE – Begins with physical contact that causes bodily harm to another, such as beating, pushing, punching, slapping, pinching, choking, snatching, dragging, etc. Unfortunately, this is by far the most familiar form of abuse, as well as the most recognizable and judged form. Still, with physical abuse, we are able to heal, but with the other forms of abuse, such as the mental or emotional traumas attached, it may last a lifetime.

To be clear, the discipline of a child and physical abuse are totally different. How so? With our child, as long as bodily harm is not caused, discipline is coming out of love, and the child has an understanding of WHY discipline is necessary, we are in alignment with what God has in mind. *"He who spares his rod hates his son, but he who loves him disciplines him promptly."* Proverbs 13:24.

Anything other than this, or outright abusing someone to control them, is always attached to mental or emotional abuse, even appearing as a physical outcome. Therefore, in the Eye of God, this creates a double-edged sword of resolvable issues that must be dealt with accordingly, *As It Pleases Him.*

MENTAL ABUSE – Begins with bullying, intimidating, manipulating, projecting, blaming, harassing, spying, insulting, or creating a hostile environment to brainwash someone. Most often, this is accomplished by making the abusee think they are crazy or are at fault for the situation, circumstance, or event.

A mentally abusive person may also make threats to hurt or kill themselves, the person's family, and friends. They may also make vain threats to ruin a person financially, destroy personal property, spread gossip, or reveal a person's innermost secrets through mind games.

Although mind control takes a little longer to accomplish, it has the most profound impact that goes unrecognized by the abusee. However, the mentally abused person is most recognized by their actions, reactions, thoughts, beliefs, words, and fears; consequently, they have a double impact as an abuser and the abusee, to say the least. In so many words, a mentally abused person is destined to knowingly or unknowingly become an abuser if they do not receive some sort of intervention, especially Divine Intervention, *As It Pleases God.*

EMOTIONAL ABUSE – Begins with verbal abuse, such as name-calling, criticizing, belittling, embarrassment, manipulation, coercion, ignoring, or extreme humiliation. This low-level or underlying tactic may also include the deprivation of affection, deprivation of attention, deprivation of approval, bullying, or outright rejection.

The intentional grafting of this root often occurs when the abuser refuses to accept responsibility for anything. Then again, it may appear when they find fault in the abusee to make themselves feel superior, create a façade as if they cannot do anything wrong, or they are justified in their actions.

Most often, with emotional abuse, the abuser knows exactly what they are doing. How? It is premeditated behavior. Simply put, they have to make a conscious effort to think of things to reject, manipulate, coerce, hurt, or bring harm to the abusee.

Defamation of character is definitely a thought-out behavior, setting the Law of Reciprocity in motion faster than any other form of abuse. Why? This behavior is not an instant response, reaction, or reflex. It takes work, going through varying channels such as thinking, planning, positioning, and executing.

Unbeknown to most, it carries the most amount of penalty in the Eye of God, even if we do not put our paws on someone physically. How is this possible? The mental and emotional imprints and seeds are left behind as a root, creating rotten fruit when we had the same opportunity to plant a good seed and chose not to do so.

SPIRITUAL ABUSE – Begins when a person uses the Bible to manipulate others, to control others, or to use scripture to justify their actions through misrepresentation. This behavior also may incorporate the use of negativity or cause ill will through bad-mouthing, negative prayers, or negative thinking of those who do not know what they are doing.

To clarify this whitewashed form of abuse, those who couldn't care less about what they are doing often use prayers, rituals, or spells to control others through the use of Black Magic, Wicca, Voodoo/Hoodoo, Santeria, word curses, etc., using the Bible to play dirty.

Although we may not talk about Spiritual Abuse much or deny the use of such practices, but there is a reason why the fortune teller, occultist, and the wolves in sheep's clothing stay in business. Most often, it is through our ignorance, greed, or selfishness. This type of behavior has been around since the beginning of time, and it is not going anywhere! Therefore, we must learn how to equip ourselves for warfare, *As It Pleases God* and not with what pleases us. Why? *"For we do not wrestle against flesh and blood, but against principalities, against powers, against the rulers of the darkness of this age, against spiritual hosts of wickedness in the heavenly places."* Ephesians 6:12.

ECONOMIC ABUSE – Begins when a person uses money as a form of punishment or when an individual makes their partner beg for basic necessities. It could fall under overspending as well; however, extreme abuse in this area comes about when a person demands their partner give them their whole paycheck, spends the whole paycheck on wayward activities, or counts the money down to the exact penny. This behavior also includes keeping a mate from seeking employment or making them suffer financially so they can depend on them.

SEXUAL ABUSE – Begins when an individual is forced to have sex or indulge in explicit behavior that degrades them. This is also applicable to being treated like a sex object, solicited for sex, withholding sex, or accusations of affairs. In today's time, this is most often used in open relationships, controlled relationships, hidden relationships, or friends-with-benefits relationships.

We have gotten to the point that sexual abuse has become second-nature, especially when men and women are giving themselves away for power, money, and status. It is often said that everyone has a price, which is true to a certain extent, because we are mere flesh and blood.

Why would we abuse someone to the point where they would have to choose to be abused because of money, power, or status? The reasoning will vary from person to person, situation to situation, trauma to trauma, culture to culture, and so on. The bottom line is that God sees and knows all.

"There is no creature hidden from His sight, but all things are naked and open to the eyes of Him to whom we must give account." Hebrews 4:13.

The one thing I have found is that abuse occurs in every culture and at every socioeconomic level. Regardless of where we are in life, we will think 1 of 4 things:

- ☐ We will think abuse will never happen to us.
- ☐ We will think we deserve to be abused.
- ☐ We will think we **do not** deserve to be abused.
- ☐ We will think we have the right to abuse.

We often believe women are more abused than men; however, I beg to differ. Men are just as abused as women; they just do not mention it because they are experts at keeping secrets.

Actually, men are more susceptible to all forms of abuse except for physical abuse. It is indeed true that more women are prone to physical abuse than men, but with all the other forms of abuse, men rank just as high, if not higher. Of course, men are not going to mention they are being emotionally abused, mentally abused, economically abused, sexually deprived and manipulated, shamed, insulted, or stalked by their wives or girlfriends.

Whether male or female, abuse is all around us: in our homes, in hostile environments abroad, in the workplace, and on social media platforms, and the list goes on. The writing is always on the wall with an abuser or an abusee. So, if we can't get away from it, we must learn and understand it to ensure we do not become the next victim.

The ultimate goal of an abuser is to seek power and precedence over something or someone. The love of power and the fear of losing it will drive an abuser to great extremes. Here are a few things we need to know:

- [ ] The pains of the past produce the problems of today.
- [ ] The victim, as a child, often grows up to be victimized as an adult.
- [ ] Abuse victims often become perfectionists and high achievers.
- [ ] Those who are often abused become abusers.
- [ ] Abuse victims feel they are to blame.
- [ ] Headaches, asthma, body pain, and eating disorders are often symptoms of abuse or emotional problems.
- [ ] Abusers are often respected people.
- [ ] Angry people sometimes blame others for their misfortunes.
- [ ] A negative self-image stems from real or perceived deprivation or rejection, as well as abuse.
- [ ] Sexual abuse often leads to sexual problems, promiscuity, or secret acts of prostitution.
- [ ] Suppressed emotions often lead to physical symptoms.
- [ ] Forgiveness is essential for emotional healing.

Abuse is unacceptable, regardless of what type it is. Whether we are married, unmarried, or anything in between, when there is an ITCH from within, we will often ask ourselves:

- [ ] What's wrong with me?
- [ ] What have I done so wrong?

- [ ] Why do I keep attracting these types of relationships?
- [ ] Will I ever meet the right person?

Our conditioning or programming from our childhood experiences determines the level of anger we exhibit, our level of self-esteem, and our level of security. They amazingly work together regardless of whether we were raised by both parents, neglected by a parent, mistreated by a parent, lost a parent during childhood, abandoned, or whether we had surrogate parents or were raised by an institution, positive and negative programming will take place.

For the individuals whose parents were physically or emotionally absent, rest assured, there will be self-esteem issues of unworthiness, unlovability, or insecurity that must be worked on consistently. When dealing with these types of issues, we very well may spend years unlearning, relearning, or getting over some things. Still, we must truly understand the point of origin or *Get To The Root* of whatever with whomever, especially if we want to really understand who we are as a person, *As It Pleases God.*

Why is it imperative to *Get To The Root* of our issues or setbacks? Negative experiences, traumas, and hurts produce baggage or debauched fruits, even if we pretend we are all good. Plus, with every piece of baggage or rotting fruit, the ITCH gets stronger and more frequent. Therefore, we must find a way to refuse the negative baggage and fruits we do not want to keep in our repertoire. Why? Pruning must occur when growing great in the Eye of God. Really? Yes, really! *"Every branch in Me that does not bear fruit He takes away; and every branch that bears fruit He prunes, that it may bear more fruit."* John 15:2.

Improving ourselves is at its best when we are consciously able to see beyond the negative to get to the positive. We are in control over our lives, and having a positive attitude and mindset will definitely give us the upper hand in doing so.

On the other hand, we also have a glitch in our system as well. How so? When we feel as if we are in control, we will always feel a sense of wanting or achieving more, which is only natural for us. Still, it can also be detrimental if we do not interject self-control or leave God out of our equational efforts altogether.

How do we recognize the glitch? We must query ourselves, exposing our truth, heart posture, mindset, character, and fruits. For example, if we had the desires of our hearts, what would we do with it, that, or them? Would we accomplish more, waste more time, watch more TV, and find more unproductive things to cram into our time? We all want more money, but if we had it, what would we do? Would we save it, invest it, buy more stuff, accrue more bills, brag, or help others?

We all want more of something, and for this reason, we need to know what we are going to do with the things we are hoping and praying for. If not, more than likely, what God has for us, we may not recognize it when it is presented. Why? It will never be packaged the way we think. Only the counterfeits are packaged, appealing to our senses, idiosyncrasies, lust, hangups, or biases, nullifying our conscience, common sense, and discerning faculties. Really? Yes, really?

God gives us seeds, roots, and fruits to work with to Spiritually Till our own ground, perfecting our talents, creativity, passion, senses, discernment, conscience, and skills. On the other hand, our adversary will present us with the fully loaded nonparticipatory package without accounting for the cost on the front end, but paying dearly on the back end.

It is okay to want and to become more. Still, we must ensure a positive change occurs within our mind first, *As It Pleases God*, without allowing negative people, places, and things into our headspace. If not, we will find ourselves wanting them for the wrong reasons. Besides, when we can deal with the negativity in our lives, we are better able to make wise decisions while developing great strategies on how to turn a superficial negative into a positive.

According to the Heavenly of Heavens, you will always have the potential to make your dream or passion happen as long as you do not give up on yourself. How is this possible? Everything you need is already within. If you do not know this, it is time to get in the know, *As It Pleases God*.

Spiritually, when you learn how to pray effectively, while using scripture to back it up, you will then position yourself to become strong emotionally. As a result, you are better able to deal with the negativity surrounding you and still move forward in excellence.

When *Getting To The Root* in this lifetime, you are the best positive you that you have, so make the most of it. Of course, I know you hear about this positive hoopla all the time, and I write as if it's so easy. I know personally it's not always easy, especially when you are going through something. Still, the freedom of love will change everything if you believe and become your authentic self.

So, stay with *The Psalms Doctor* on this journey, and we will prepare together with the *Emotional Truth*, *As It Pleases God*.

PRAYER

Father, My God, in the Name of Jesus, I am *Getting To The Root* of what really matters in my life, according to my Predestined Blueprint. I pray that You help me to love myself and others the way You love, with no strings attached. Moreover, if I have found favor in Your sight, please allow Your Divine Love to flow through my veins to ensure Your Divine Love is freely pumped into the lives of others.

When I feel the sting of hurt or rejection, allow it to bounce off me as if nothing happened. And, for this reason, I ask in the Mighty Name of Jesus, You strengthen my heart to deal with the emotional woes of life. Although I may not receive love in return from others, I know that Your grace is sufficient enough that I will not feel the sting of rejection, manipulation, or abuse.

Father, as You cleanse and purify my mind, body, soul, and spirit, *As It Pleases You*, prune all negativity and ill will and replace them with the Fruits of the Spirit, Christlike Character with power, passion, and purpose. For this, O' Lord, I give thanks to You, and Your praises will be continually on my lips. Amen.

SCRIPTURE READING:

PSALMS 8
PSALMS 10
PSALMS 37

CHAPTER 3

EMOTIONAL TRUTH

As we continue to breathe the breath of life, emotions will flow through our veins whether we like it or not. Our *Emotional Truths* are a vital part of our being, and we try to block them out. Unfortunately, it is through the blocking of our emotions that causes us the greatest pain and losses, stunting our growth, *As It Pleases God*. What is the big deal? In order to truly embrace the essence of blissful living, we must understand and respect our emotions. If not, due to our adaptive nature, we will find ourselves emotionally bound, yoked, or soul-tied without realizing it or thinking we are right in our own eyes.

When unveiling the *Emotional Truth*, if we take a moment to look around us, we will find everyone is trying to knowingly or unknowingly fill a void from within. Then again, they may have a massive cover-up appeasing the human psyche. How is this possible, especially as a Believer, having it going on and wanting for nothing? We are created to hide behind something or someone as a cover-up.

Adam and Eve got this party started in the Garden of Eden, and nothing has changed since. We were born into a natural domain of whitewashing unless we query ourselves, *As It Pleases God*. Simply put, we must ask ourselves (the psyche) the hard questions to extract the *Emotional Truth* about the what, when, where, how, and why regarding our thoughts and feelings, transforming it into Emotional Intelligence without falling into the trap of an emotional stupor.

Here is the difference: Emotional Intelligence refers to the ability to recognize, understand, and manage our emotions, as well as the emotions of others. In addition, it plays a vital role in interpersonal relationships, communication, and decisions, making our people skills impeccable.

In the Eye of God, possessing high Emotional Intelligence, *As It Pleases Him*, helps us handle stressful situations effectively without bottling up or dumping emotions. Why must we add Him? It aids in regulating our *Emotional Truth*, allowing us to be authentic, empathize with others, and build stronger connections with those around us amid differences.

On the other hand, emotional stupors cause the best of us to hate ourselves, start looking for love in all the wrong places, go overboard to please others, or simply try too hard to make someone love us through manipulation, control, or lies.

Although everyone will have their own set of issues to deal with, when we have the facts about why we are doing what we do, we are better able to find solutions, *As It Pleases God*, not as it pleases ourselves.

Nevertheless, throughout my many years of meeting great people, I met this beautiful young lady named Kinsey. She was absolutely gorgeous. After speaking with her for several hours, I found this beautiful woman to be the most insecure woman I had ever met. She constantly criticized herself, her abilities, and her life. I could not believe such a phenomenal woman could be so negative, hating the life that God had so gracefully blessed her with.

After expressing sincere compassion for Kinsey, she began to open up to me. She explained how she was born as a result of an affair. She went on to tell me how her mother had a serious crush on this married guy, and the only way to keep this man in her life was to get pregnant, so she did. After Kinsey's birth, her father kept it a secret from his wife for about seven years.

Kinsey's mom got tired of her baby daddy using her to satiate his fancy with their midnight rendezvous. Plus, she was exhausted with his lies, being on an emotional rollercoaster, and waiting for him to leave his wife. So, she decided to execute her *Emotional Truth* by taking matters into her own hands to break up his home by telling his wife about the affair and his secret child.

As a result, this home wrecker gets bold enough to approach another man's wife publicly, with her pre-vaseline face, as if she had papers on a married man privately. More importantly, God was nowhere in this equation; she threw all of her Emotional Intelligence in the trash, hoping to finally win his love. Nonetheless, these two women got into a big fight, and this altercation became like the WWE for women. They were snatching wigs, throwing rocks, and breaking windows while this sorry man stood back, watched, and laughed as his third side chick recorded them to post on YouTube.

These two women pulled out every trick in the book to keep Kinsey's dad. As a result of the fight, the wife won. She made her husband cut off all contact with Kinsey's mom as if she were doing something big or making a statement. Even though she had every right to make this request, she did not realize his third side chick got all the credit for exposing their foolery, as she moved up in ranking to number two.

Kinsey's mom was so angry that she lost her married man to his wife that she began to blame her child. Her anger became so deep-rooted and dark that she refused to seek medical attention for the lump on her head. When we talk about love being blind, how blind can a person become when attempting to take something or someone not belong to them?

After the ordeal, she could not stand to look at the child they had created together. So, she made Kinsey feel as if she were the scum of the earth. Her mother would verbally tell her how much she hated her, as her sisters constantly told her she was so ugly. As a result, Kinsey became a loner, blocking out everyone, including her childhood friends.

After being taunted for years in anguish, Kinsey wallowed in extreme rage and resentment toward her family, continuing this negative cycle. As her anger began to boil over, she would take it out on animals. She openly admitted to trying to kill her cat, abusing her dog, and choking her hamster to avoid doing something to her mom and sisters after they beat her up and cut her long hair. I was literally in tears as she shared her story with me, but I had to allow her to tell her testimony.

One day, her mother got so tired of looking at her that she took her and dropped her off on her father's doorstep with one bag of clothes. Kinsey cried for days. Her stepmom did not care for her, and she turned her daughters against her as well. It was as if Kinsey was taken out of the pot and placed into the frying pan. Her stepmom was the meanest woman in town, who had to control everything, including her husband.

If Kinsey wanted to stay in the house, she had to earn her keep. She had to clean behind everyone like a little housegirl. She cleaned windows, scrubbed floors, washed clothes, took out the garbage, etc., while her step-sisters did nothing but go to school, eat, play, and go to church with zero responsibilities. Unfortunately, this love-starved child grew up associating love with cleaning up. If she wanted to get attention, she cleaned up, causing her to become an obsessive-compulsive cleaning fanatic.

Kinsey never learned how to love, nor did she care about learning how to do so. As she adapted to her lifestyle, she was okay with becoming complacent with her self-defiant mindset. As the years clicked by, she began to hate her biological mother, sisters, step-mom, and step-sisters, more and more, for how they treated her as she continued to relive her past. Kinsey could not get over the feelings associated with being unwanted, abused, misused, and mistreated. So, as she grew older, she began to hate herself more and more. It got so bad in her emotional stupor that she would unconsciously do things to make people dislike her.

As this negativity and self-sabotage became normal for Kinsey, if someone appeared to take an interest, she would push them away with her insecure rhetoric. Why would she push people away? She did not feel as if she was worthy of being loved, nor was she able to communicate effectively. As a result, she was not able to express herself normally. This consistent barrage of self-doubt created a lens through which she viewed relationships, leading her to believe that any interest shown to her was undeserved or superficial.

When someone would take the time to express care or concern, her instinct was to deflect and dismantle those budding connections with her insecure rhetoric. Kinsey's internal dialogue was steeped in atrocious negativity. The negative chatter from within her was constantly convincing her that affection from others was a mistake, or even worse, a superficial façade. This mindset not only undermined her self-esteem but also distorted her mental playback and her perception of people and healthy relationships.

Kinsey's story sheds light on this painful cycle, illustrating how deep-seated insecurities can lead to self-sabotage and isolation. Sadly, emotional and mental abuse have consumed this young lady's life to the point of no return. Today, Kinsey is still fighting with her family on both sides. She still hates them, and they hate her ways. Sadly, she also absolutely refuses to forgive her family members or repent of her contributions to the situation under any circumstances.

Kinsey has gone through an extensive amount of counseling. Still, she refuses to let go of the past and willfully holds on to the trauma by constantly rehashing and leveraging it against her family for justification of her behaviors.

I explained to her she was able to **Get the Information to Change Herself Out of the Bible**, but she couldn't care less about the Bible and God. I would think to myself, 'What a life to live without having God in it!' I was amazed at her desire to wallow without becoming *The Psalms Doctor* over her own life by simply reading scriptures, which turned out to be not a viable option for her.

How is it that we have our blessings at our fingertips and become so blind to their power? When all we have to do is learn how to love ourselves enough to embrace all life has in store. We are so blessed and do not realize it. Every day we wake up, we are blessed to see another day; therefore, we must not allow the past to cloud our judgment and our desire to live a fulfilled lifestyle.

PRAYER

Restore me, O' Lord! Please grant me emotional stability during the trials and challenges of life. Help me to remain calm and composed in the face of adversity. Strengthen me with Your love and guidance so that I may navigate difficult situations with ease in my *Emotional Truth*. I pray for wisdom to make sound decisions and the courage to face my fears and overcome my adversities. May Your Divine Presence bring peace to my heart and comfort to my soul.

Father, my Lord, I come to You seeking emotional intelligence and wisdom to navigate the complexities of life. Please grant me the ability to understand and manage my thoughts, feelings, desires, and hangups, as well as the tenacity to deal with the emotions of others. *As It Pleases You*, help me communicate effectively and empathetically and respond to challenging situations with patience and grace.

May I cultivate a deep sense of self-awareness, identifying and regulating my thoughts and feelings healthily and constructively with a keen sense of intuition.

As You guide me on the right path, *As It Pleases You*, help me to make wise decisions in alignment with my Predestined Blueprint. May I be filled with love, kindness, and compassion towards myself and others. Thank you for your boundless love and support and for blessing me with the gift of life, in the Name of Jesus. Amen.

SCRIPTURE READING:

PSALMS 119
PSALMS 126
PSALMS 143

CHAPTER 4

GENETIC MAKEUP

Do you take your *Genetic Makeup* into consideration? Do you take your Bloodline seriously? Have you considered that your Genetic Makeup has something to do with your Divine Purpose? God has placed us in a specific family for a reason, and if we fail to learn, understand, and become better, stronger, and wiser, we may create a disservice to ourselves.

Throughout my journey in life, I have found that the key to living a fulfilled life is to develop a relationship with our Heavenly Father first, *Spirit to Spirit*, a relationship with ourselves, and then on to building a relationship with others. If we get this out of order, chaos will soon follow in religion, in a relationship, in our ability to give and receive love, or in life, with a constant cycle of déjà vu.

Without building relationships in this order, our Genetic Makeup will not unveil itself completely, even if we possess man-made documents. Why? Man-made does not equate to a Spiritual Analysis of our Genetic Makeup, *As It Pleases God*. No one has the Heavenly Specifics of our Predestined

Blueprint outside of God and the one who is carrying it. Although He has designed people to help, prepare, nurture, or guide us, no one can replicate our fingerprint, eyeprint, mindprint, thoughtprint, or purposeprint without our participatory involvement or the Spiritual Tilling of our own ground.

God has set a specific order in the Universe. For example, in the morning, we will never see the sunset before the sunrise; we will never see the sunrise from the west or the sunset in the east. The day we see this happening, RUN! Why? We have a serious problem, and Divine Order has become chaotically corrupted.

What does chaos have to do with anything? Chaos is all around us, and it is in our *Genetic Makeup*, even if we think it is not. Most often, it is hidden...but it does not mean it does not exist. What can we do about it? Absolutely nothing, right? Wrong. The key to overcoming the chaos is to understand it, *As It Pleases God.*

What is there to understand about chaos? Unbeknown to most, chaos is what makes our gene pool work. Chaotic conception. Chaotic Birth. Chaotic challenges. The bottom line is that the chaos makes our *Genetic Makeup* stronger or weaker by the choices we make. Although some like chaos, some do not like it, and some are conditioned to tolerate it. Then again, we have some who are educated in an area of their lives, keeping them paralyzed, not knowing which way to turn. In the Eye of God, we do not have to become a victim of it, them, or that.

Some time ago, a few friends introduced me to this family, which literally amazed me. It made my issues with my family minuscule. I could not believe this family functioned in such a way; actually, it made me appreciate my family even more.

Nevertheless, I needed to find out how this family got to this state, and boy, did I get a wake-up call. Here is what I found: This family was cursed back in the early 1900s. William and Jallee got married at a very young age; although they were both immature, it did not stop them from having a family. Every year, it seemed as if Jallee was pushing out a baby; in total, she had nine girls and four boys. William loved having a big family, but there was one problem—he was broke. He had very little money to support them. Even though they ate the leftovers from the restaurant where he worked, it wasn't enough. He had to do something.

One day, William had this bright idea. The sinister plot he presumed was a bright idea, which was that he could make more than enough money with his nine daughters. So, William began to prostitute his daughters for money, food, water, and moonshine. Then, he used his sons to keep the books on their sisters, keep an inventory of goods, and sell what they had left over. Jallee pleaded with him to stop prostituting his children, but he was adamant about not going to bed hungry ever again. Yes, William was a cook by day and a true hustler by night—living a well-to-do life.

His daughters grew up to hate him. As they began to have babies from customers, he would sell the newborns and the baby's milk to willing buyers. William became ruthless by the day; he would sell anything he could get his hands on, except for his wife. He knew that his wife held all of his secrets, and he knew that he needed her to cook, clean, and take care of his kids because they were a viable source of revenue. So he dared not cross her.

What his precious wife, Jallee, did not know was that her clickety-clank husband kept another family across town on the other side of the tracks. All the years she allowed him to prostitute her children and sell her grandbabies, he kept another wife across town with two daughters in private school who knew nothing about them or his raggedy, pimping lifestyle.

After Jallee found out about his prestigious uptown family, there was never a peaceful moment in the house until the day she died. Some believed she died from a broken heart, and others said she could no longer live with her conscience. But one thing they do know is undeniable chaos ruled the family from that day forward.

As the children grew older, they would fight each other like they were enemies. They were ruthless like their father; they did not respect each other, and they couldn't care less about respecting other people. Leslie, in particular, was the spitting image of her father. She was indeed a hustler by trade and a prostitute every now and then; however, she refused to prostitute her children.

Leslie could make more than enough money selling moonshine and running numbers. Living the fast life of drinking, smoking, and having fun with men, she was hell on wheels. This woman had a mouth on her; she cursed like a sailor and would do almost anything for money. Her kids began to follow in her footsteps, doing almost anything for money as well.

One day, Leslie scored really big by running her numbers, and her oldest daughter, Lily, asked her for a loan. She then cursed her daughter out and said, "You have a money-maker between your legs; go use it and stop asking me for money!" Her daughter was appalled by her mom telling her to do what she vowed never to do to her children. After the shock subsided, she took her mom's advice anyway.

Lily began to follow in her mom's footsteps, doing anything to make money. She became so jealous of her mom that she had someone rob her. This attack was the ultimate betrayal for her mom, and when she realized who was robbing her, she fought back. The guy could not risk getting caught or exposing Lily, so he shot her, killing her instantly.

Of course, Lily has to live with that dreadful memory for the rest of her life as betrayal continues through her bloodline. Now, Lily has turned to legally suing people with fictitious claims, extorting over $500,000.00 in claims thus far. Her children are following in her footsteps as well, suing, robbing, and undercover prostitution. This family will do anything for money, and they do not feel as if they have ever done anything wrong.

Lily has this one daughter in particular; she is the greatest con artist ever. She knows how to cheat you out of a dime when you only have a nickel; she's just that good. Actually, she picked up where her mother and grandmother left off; she was determined to do what she needed to do to survive.

A history of sexual, mental, and emotional abuse has plagued this family beyond what we could ever imagine. As a result of this genetic chaos, this plague has not stopped as of yet; it's already in its 5th generation.

The last update I have of this family is that William died a year after Leslie was killed. Lily is waiting to cash in on the insurance policies she has on her children and grandchildren while living off the money from her last lawsuit of $200,000.00.

This family is still permeated with prostitution, identity theft, bribery, robbery, and suing on a more sophisticated level. The power of manipulation has clouded this family's way of thinking, and I believe they really enjoy the chaos.

If they really wanted to change, they could, if they would just put their past behind them, exercise the power of forgiveness, fast, and pray. It would break this generational curse. I really wonder how long this family will continue in their folly; however, I could not help but reflect on Luke 6:44, which says, *"For every tree is known by its own fruit. For men do not gather figs from thorns, nor do they gather grapes from a bramble bush."* Change comes when we make the necessary sacrifices to put dead or chaotic things behind us. What's in the past is in the past! There is no need to bury ourselves in the things of old. Actually, it is the things of old that keep our heads buried in the sand of mental anguish. Furthermore, when we allow ourselves to become too mentally entangled in someone or something, rest assured that emotional bondage will soon follow like a thief in the night. Yes, most often, it will take more than we are willing to give.

Our willingness to put away dead things gives us the power to cope, forgive, let go, and eliminate our sensitivities to being misunderstood. Every day, in conjunction with the use of *The Psalms Doctor* provides us with an opportunity to live better than we did the day before. When we allow ourselves to live in victory, we then open the door to succeed in places we never knew existed. More importantly, it causes our *Genetic Makeup* to work together for our good instead of to our detriment.

Putting things behind you will definitely give you a boost of confidence to move forward in the Spirit of Excellence, especially when others are looking at the impossibilities at hand. God can and will do exceedingly and abundantly above all you can ask or think as long as you trust, forgive, and believe He can and will.

Amid any form of chaos, confusion, or atrocity, God will always provide Divine Wisdom inside of it. However, it is your responsibility to Spiritually Till your own ground, extracting and converting it into what it was designed to become, similar to a diamond in the rough.

PRAYER

Father, my God, in the Name of Jesus, my soul and *Genetic Makeup* pants for You. You are a breath of living water, quenching my inner thirst with the power of forgiveness.

I hereby forgive anyone who has trespassed against, deceived, angered, provoked, hurt, upset, offended, used, or sinned against me in any way, shape, or form. Before I go any further in this healing process, I forgive myself. I invoke the Spirit of Forgiveness to permeate into the depths of my soul, releasing me from anything or anyone, causing me to hoard secret acts of revenge or retaliation.

As the Spirit of Forgiveness is upon me, My God, allow the words of my mouth and the meditations of my heart to become holy and acceptable in Your sight as I embark upon this journey. Father, please allow me to be forgiven by others for any known or unknown, accidental or willful, intentional or unintentional, sinful actions, whether by word, deed, thoughts, creed, or attitude. If I have brought about any ungodly action or reaction that's outside of Your will, let me change in ways that make it easy for me to avoid paths of hurtfulness to others.

As forgiveness takes place from within me, Lord, allow me to change my ways and break any generational curse to ensure Your divine grace and mercy radiate through my actions, reactions, and attitude. Regardless of what others think about the power of my ability to forgive, I know that beyond a shadow of a doubt, You are guiding my every footstep. Besides, to be guided by Your presence means unforgiveness cannot take up residence where You reside.

Thank You for creating me in Your image and for giving me unique qualities and abilities, making me who I am. Please help me use these gifts for the betterment of myself and others to fulfill Your purpose, in the name of Jesus. Amen.

SCRIPTURE READING:

PSALMS 25
PSALMS 105

CHAPTER 5

REMOVE THE MASK

Do you know who you are? Do you know why you exist? Are you hiding your authentic self? Are you stuck in pretend mode? Do you fear being you? Regardless of who you are, what you are doing, or why you are doing it, God has placed a Clarion Call to *Remove The Mask*. According to the Heavenly of Heavens, He is demanding authenticity from you, us, and them.

Life has a way of rubbing us the wrong way, especially when we want something or someone badly, and are unwilling to add God into the equation or put in the work, *As It Pleases Him*. What does God have to do with being rubbed the wrong way? When rubbed in the right or wrong way with Him involved in our lives, *As It Pleases Him*, we can create a win-win regardless.

On the other hand, when we omit Him, most often, we have something to hide, we are masking something, or we do not want our skeletons to fall out of the closet. So, we usually opt not to play ball with the Master because we are required to play by the rulebook.

I realized this when a bunch of my friends came over to my house for a Pillow Talk session about *Removing The Masks*. As we began to tell wild stories about ourselves, this new attendee, Macy, had the most unusual story about 'The Mask of Insanity.'

Macy's mask of insanity began at the early age of 16 when she ran off on an escapade with her childhood sweetheart. He pretended to love her, and she gave in to his charm, not realizing that she would become pregnant. That's where she put on her 1st mask; she hid her pregnancy up until her 7th month. By this time, it was too late for an abortion. Her mom was furious, and she was not willing to take care of another child.

Macy had to make a decision. She decided to keep her child, hoping the father would remain with her. After telling her mom about the decision, her mom put her out of her house. She called her boyfriend to tell him what happened, and he yelled at her, saying, "That's not my child." However, he wasn't saying that when he was doing the do! It is amazing how quickly he forgets about his sweet nothings, especially when having to account for the cost of an escapade going sourly south with a child on its way into this world.

Macy wandered the streets for a few days and finally ended up in a shelter until she had the baby. She felt so alone, betrayed, and foolish, with no place to go, until she met this young man who promised her the world on one condition. He wasn't going to take care of another man's child, and she agreed he should not have to because she did not ask for a baby, to be a mother, or to become homeless.

In survival mode, a few days later, Macy took her newborn baby boy to his grandparents' house to visit, and she never went back for him. She had to wear the mask of the disgrace of leaving her child to be with another man, but it was a price she was willing to pay.

Eventually, she got over it as she became pregnant with her new man, as they lived in their own little façade of temporary happiness. After her newness had worn off, she realized he was an abuser, alcoholic, and drug addict. While pregnant, he began to beat her for everything, even for looking at him the wrong way. She lived under an enormous amount of guilt, pressure, and resentment. Macy sat at home all day thinking about how she gave up her son for this man, only to receive beatings in return. The more she thought about it, the angrier she became.

One rainy day, her boyfriend came in really toasted, stumbling all over the house looking for the cigarettes he had bought two days ago. He knew they were in the house somewhere, so he asked Macy to help look for them, and she refused. She did not feel like searching around the house for his smokes. He became furious with her, knocking her out of the chair onto the cold floor with no consideration that she was pregnant. As she stood up, he began to beat her like there was no tomorrow. Macy thought he was going to kill her and her unborn child, so she grabbed a lamp, hit him with it, and ran out of the house.

She ran to a friend's house, hoping that she didn't kill him; however, after receiving a few stitches, her boyfriend came looking for her, begging her to come back home, and she did. Things went okay for a couple of weeks, but his drug habits became worse. He began to shoot up.

While still pregnant, Macy met Rick. He was a pretty decent guy who worked hard and made a pretty good salary. She had a fear of living on the streets again, and she was willing to do anything not to go back. After seeing Rick for a few months, she felt as if she had hit the jackpot. However, she had to figure out a way to break away from her boyfriend, because she knew he was not going to give up easily. So she waited for the opportune moment to execute a plan.

Macy knew he liked shooting up, so she put water in his needle. When he shot up that night, it stopped his heart. She called the paramedics as if she had done nothing wrong. Nor did she tell them the truth.

Nevertheless, they got him back to breathing again; however, he suffered damage to the brain, which left him in a wheelchair for the rest of his life. There wasn't an investigation because he had a history of drug use, overdosing, and an extensive criminal history. They felt as if he was no longer a threat to society, and he was better off in a wheelchair.

Macy got what she wanted, but she had to put on the 2nd mask. She could never let anyone know what she did, especially Rick, her new victim. Of course, Rick wasn't a saint, but he had money, and he was willing to take care of Macy. This was her ticket to freedom, and she was not going to allow anyone to take it away from her.

After having a child with her previous boyfriend, she immediately became pregnant with Rick's child. He was so excited. He was like a kid in a candy store. After she had locked Rick down, they got married. She had her mask on for a few years until the lust of her flesh got the best of her.

Macy did not love Rick as a wife should, and for some odd reason, Rick knew it. However, he had a family; she got what she wanted, he got what he wanted, and there was no reason to rock the boat, right? Wrong. Macy got buck-wild. She had a thing for men in uniforms; therefore, she fell head over heels in love with this married police officer. Cory, the police officer, was only looking for a fling while Macy was looking for a new man. Cory played Macy like a little fiddle, as she was blinded by her own lust of greed.

After carrying on with the relationship for years, Cory asked Macy to set up one of her friends from high school in an undercover drug bust. In the name of love, she agreed. She went undercover, sparking a sexual relationship with this guy while getting all of his personal information. She wore a wire, took pictures, etc. Macy went all out like she was an undercover cop with zero compensation.

Why was she doing all of this? All of this was done for Cory's love. Eventually, her friend got busted and went to prison. Like clockwork, Cory, the married man, dumped her. Macy was devastated, crying for months. Now, to add insult to injury, after betraying a friend, acting like a detective, and getting thrown to the curb, the friend she set up was killed in prison. What a life to live, especially when having the same opportunity to mind her own business and take care of her husband and family, right? Wrong. She became more vindictive, putting on her 3rd mask.

Macy is a married woman, and her husband does not have a clue about the type of woman he is dealing with. However, she was not going to stop until she made Cory feel the hurt and embarrassment she had to endure, making her feel like a fool for loving him.

One day, when the timing was right, Macy came up with a plan. She sparked a relationship with Cory's best friend, who was also married. Somehow, she got him on her good side to arrange a ménage à trois with him and another police officer. After the event, they talked about her so badly. Cory was so humiliated by her lascivious acts that he could not stand to look at her ever again.

Macy got her revenge, and she was on the prowl, looking for her next victim, while Rick took the time to raise the children. It's sad to say, but being a mother was not her highest priority; she wanted to experience the fairytale romance of catching her Mr. Right.

After searching for years, ignoring her family, Macy found him. Actually, she met her match. It was love at first sight! She was looking for love, and he was looking for a victim. He told her everything she wanted to hear. Her Mr. Right spoiled her with fancy gifts, he took her to fancy restaurants, and he painted a picture of love she had always dreamt about. He became her world as she lost interest in her husband, her kids, and her motherly responsibilities.

After becoming the lovebirds of the century, Mr. So-called Right convinced her to move out, leaving everything behind. The henpecked Macy undoubtedly packed her bags to move in with him, while leaving her kids with Rick and abandoning her family for the illusion of love.

Macy did not realize she was living the dream...she had the love of her husband, the love of her children, the love of her friends, a good job, financial stability, and living in her dream home...she had it all, but for some reason, her reality was not enough.

Being that nothing was ever good enough for Macy, she planned on divorcing Rick and marrying Mr. Right to live the fairytale dream. She did not realize she had been planting seeds from the ripe old age of 16, and her seeds were getting ready to break ground.

As she lived a single life for about six months, her children became traumatized and devastated because they realized she was not coming back. They could not believe their mother left them behind for another man. Of course, Rick was angry, but he still wanted his wife back. He and the children begged her to come back, but she said, "She needed to live her life." She filed for divorce in hopes of marrying Mr. Right.

After the divorce was final, she asked Mr. Right, "When are we getting married?" He said, "Never." She asked, "Why?" He said, "You want me to marry you, so you can leave me like you left your husband and children!" She was stunned. She left her husband for an empty promise. She burned the bridges with her now ex-husband and her children. How could she possibly go back? How could Mr. Right become Mr. Wrong?

Mr. Wrong had her right where he wanted her. That is DESPERATE. He knew once she became desperate, she would do anything for him. And he was right! He began to brainwash her into thinking he was the only person in the world who loved her. He cut her off from her family and friends while he began to do a good job on her mentally and emotionally. Sadly, her conscience began to work on the other side.

Macy was an emotional wreck! She felt as if God was punishing her for her past, but she could not find a way to ask God to forgive her. As she wallowed, she became more desperate. Mr. Wrong's goal was to turn Macy into a high-class call girl the whole time. And it was working. If she did not do it, he would beat her. This lifestyle was so embarrassing for her; she would not tell a soul. The more she did it, the easier it became for her until he brainwashed her into getting her oldest daughter back.

Macy did not want her daughter to know she was a high-class call girl, so she allowed her daughter to stay with him. Her daughter did not want to stay with Mr. Wrong because she knew what was going to happen; she could see the lust in his eyes. As Macy began to leave, her daughter ran behind her saying, "Mommy, please do not leave me. Please, Mommy, do not leave me." And she left anyway. Against her better judgment, she put her daughter in a situation to be molested by her so-called boyfriend.

Love...after all of the physical, mental, and emotional abuse given and received by Macy, she still refuses to repent, fast, pray, and ask for forgiveness; as a result, she continues on a downward spiral that hasn't stopped yet.

Just to have Mr. Wrong in her life, she sacrificed her daughter's future. She knew how he was and what he was capable of doing, but she did not care. She only thought about herself, and to her, nothing else mattered. After suffering many health problems, Mr. Wrong finally let her go because her money-maker stopped making money.

Macy is still reaping the harvest of the seeds she has sown over the years and wishes she could have a second chance at making her family work. She is alone, living her past over and over again as the fruits of her labor continue to fall at her feet, leaving her mentally insane. Rick and his daughters are living a great life by embracing the power of prayer and the hidden treasures of using *The Psalms Doctor.* As a result, it released them from becoming victims of Macy's past mistakes.

Where there's a longing, we must take into account the seeds that we have planted over the years. When we take into account what we are giving, then we are better able to understand what we are receiving. Listen, everything, and I mean everything we do, say, and think, becomes a SEED! It is up to us to determine whether or not our seeds will become positively or negatively planted, discarded, or held on to.

Life has a way of granting us the conditions in which we subconsciously choose. When given a little time, the seed that we plant can and will produce after its own kind, regardless of when, what, how, where, why, and with whom it's planted.

What about the seeds that remain unplanted? Great question, "NO HARVEST!" There are some seeds we need to plant, and there are some we should not plant in this lifetime, the next, or ever. Still, we must know the difference, *As It Pleases God.* How? Here are a few questions to ask yourself, but not limited to such:

- ☐ What are my core values and beliefs?
- ☐ What are my strengths and weaknesses?
- ☐ What are my passions and interests?
- ☐ What have been the most meaningful experiences in my life?
- ☐ What has been the most traumatizing?
- ☐ What kind of legacy do I want to leave behind?
- ☐ What am I most proud of achieving?
- ☐ What are the things that make me happy?
- ☐ What kind of impact do I want to have on the world?
- ☐ What kind of people do I admire and look up to?
- ☐ What kind of work or job would make me feel fulfilled?
- ☐ What kind of relationships do I want to have?
- ☐ What kind of lifestyle do I want to live?
- ☐ What are the things I am willing to sacrifice for?
- ☐ What are the things I am not willing to compromise on?
- ☐ What are the things I fear the most?
- ☐ What are the things that hold me back from pursuing my dreams?

- [ ] What kind of people do I want to surround myself with?
- [ ] What are the things I could do differently to improve my life?
- [ ] What are the things I need to let go of in order to move forward?
- [ ] What are the things I need to do to become the person that I want to be?
- [ ] What do I need to regraft in my life?
- [ ] How can I PLEASE God?

Your lifeline is in the seeds you are planting. From me to you, do not think for a minute you are able to supersede the laws of the land, "SEEDTIME and HARVEST." What you plant, in time, you will receive, positively or negatively.

Nonetheless, according to the Heavenly of Heavens, you are able to uproot and discard seeds planted through the regrafting of your attitude, actions, words, thoughts, and reactions, in conjunction with the use of *The Psalms Doctor*.

Today, choose your seeds carefully, as you discard the negative seeds intentionally or unintentionally planted by others.

Allow God to fill you with wisdom and courage to move forward in the Spirit of Excellence. By walking faithfully and confidently, *As It Pleases Him*, He will open the Floodgates of Heaven on your behalf. Above all, *It Is Never Too Late*!

PRAYER

My Father, my God, who art in Heaven, I come to You today in prayer, asking for Your help in *Removing The Mask* I have been wearing for so long. I have been hiding my true self from the world, afraid of rejection and judgment. But I know this is not the way to live, and I ask for Your guidance in finding the courage to be myself and overcome this identity crisis I am facing.

In the name of Jesus, I feel lost and unsure of who I am and what my purpose is, so I release my fears and doubts to trust in Your love and acceptance. As I *Remove The Mask*, give me the strength to face whatever challenges may come and to stay true to who I am, no matter what. Guide me and show me the path I am meant to take, *As It Pleases You.*

Lord, forgive me for my ungratefulness or the underlying selfishness holding me back from being my authentic self. I have been taking the blessings You have bestowed upon me for granted. I am genuinely sorry. Forgive me, and I ask for Your mercy and grace. In the Name of Jesus, help me to be grateful for all You have given me, the good and the bad, the joys and the sorrows.

My God, You are my Father, Savior, Friend, and Way Maker. You know me better than anyone else. I know You have a plan and a purpose for me. I also know You love me unconditionally and want the best for me; therefore, guide me, O' Lord, in every decision I make. Please fill me with Your Holy Spirit and transform me into Your likeness as You grant me peace, joy, and hope, *As It Pleases You.*

O'Lord, give me a heart of compassion and help me to be more selfless. Thank You for Your love, guidance, protection, authenticity, and blessings, in the Name of Jesus. Amen.

SCRIPTURE READING:

PSALMS 11
PSALMS 23
PSALMS 28
PSALMS 44

CHAPTER 6

TOO LATE FOR ME

Do you feel like it is too late? Do you feel as if life has passed you by? Do you think you have already lost the race? As *The Psalms Doctor*, as long as we have breath in our bodies, *It Is Never Too Late.* Greatness does not have an expiry date. Really? Yes, really. God created the world, and He can definitely adjust His plans to save us, even if we fall short or it is at the last minute. However, we must know and understand how to woo Him, *As It Pleases Him.*

As the cycle of life has its way, it will tell us everything we need to know if we just listen. However, I advise everyone who has an ear to hear: Be cautious about developing a deaf ear to reality or the wealth of wisdom left behind. Why? If we do not listen, become disobedient, or dull, we do not know how life will teach us the lessons we MUST learn. Needless to say, I am so glad it wasn't too late for Steve. When he shared his story with me, it made me ever so grateful in the Eye of God.

Steve was considered to be an all-time Playboy. He had women for every day of the week. Actually, he enjoyed ignoring women to drive them crazy in love with him. This strategy is one of the rules men use to provoke women to chase them or spark their interest. Does it work? Yes, it works with lingering insecurities and weaknesses within the human psyche.

Here is the deal: Insecure, ignorant, or emotional games to please ourselves attract insecure people who may appear secure, causing relational trauma among the brethren. On the other hand, if we desire a well-balanced relationship, it behooves us to engage in the game of life using the Fruits of the Spirit and behaving Christlike. Why? When we play by God's Rulebook, it will naturally weed out the wolves in sheep's clothing by default, and *As It Pleases God*.

With this people skill strategy, what belongs to us will be, and what does not belong to us cannot remain. If Steve had known this, he would have approached women differently. Nevertheless, here is the story: He was out one night, swinging it high and low with no shame. One young lady who fell victim to his games said to him, "You need God in your life." He said to her, "I am God." This young lady could not believe he was so arrogant while scratching her head in dismay.

As she walked away, she said to him, "One day, you will see how much of a God you are!" Steve blew her off by saying she was too dark to be his type. Then he spat in her face, threw his drink on her, laughed at her, and continued to mingle with his type of pretty girls in the club. As this woman walked away, drenched in alcohol and human spit, he continued to mock God Almighty and had her thrown out of the club as if she were the scum of the earth.

For some reason, it seemed as if Steve hated God, and if you spoke about God, he had an excellent debate for you. Oddly enough, he actually made it his business to discredit God, the church, and the churchgoers, especially if they were broke.

Steve was ruthless when it came down to being a Christian. If you proclaimed to be abstaining from sex, he would make it his business to break you down until he got what he wanted, then move on as if you did not exist. He said women proclaim to be strong, but they are all weak and cannot keep their legs closed to a man like him.

Steve also told me that he loved the women in the church the most. He said that they are the easiest to break because they are desperate, and the only reason they go to church is to find a man who could pay their bills. So, he sold them that dream.

They gave him what he wanted, and he kicked them to the curb because they had little faith. Why? He said if they had faith, God would have told them what type of beast they were dealing with, and they would not have made him their idol. He had women crying, fighting, and depressed over him. Can you imagine giving up your goodies to a man so that he could prove that God is not your source of strength?

As Steve and I got down to the seed of this matter, it was an old, unhealed wound. As we peeled back the layers of his *Emotional Truth*, he treated women the way his mother was treated by a confident man who proclaimed to love her. As soon as the so-called God-fearing man impregnated Steve's mom, he broke up with her without any explanation.

Consequently, Steve grew up angry, frustrated, and rebellious, hating his father. Actually, Steve's father was a pulpit player who manipulated every woman in the church, including his mother. As a result, Steve's mom had to wear the burden of shame during his whole childhood, as the church members dragged her through the dirt, calling her everything but a child of God.

Although she became a well-educated woman, she never married any other man because she could not get over the pain. Steve had to watch his mother go through rejection, loneliness, and being ostracized by other women. Therefore, he made a secret promise to himself that he was going to make every woman feel the pain that his mother had to endure. As an adult, he kept his promise to himself, but it came with some serious consequences that he ignored on a daily basis.

Even though Steve had a lot of women and plenty of money, he was still lonely. He could not understand how he could have his choice of women and men on occasion and still not be fulfilled. So, instead, he began to drink and party a little more. Sadly, it did not work. He tried hanging out with his professional friends, but it still did not work. Nothing seemed to satisfy the longing from within Steve's soul.

It was so sad that behind the façade of being Mr. Fabulous Playboy, he was a lonely boy in need of SPIRITUAL HEALING. The more he played women, the bigger the longing became within his soul. The more he secretly dabbled with men on occasion, the more the longing became pits of pure shame and total regret.

He went to see his mother one day, and this old lady called him over to tell him something. He started not to go, but it would have been rude of him not to respect his elders. So he went. The lady appeared to be a little strange as she began to reach out to hold his hand. She said, "Baby, God is watching your every move. He has a calling on your life, and you will never find happiness outside of his calling. The more you run, the bigger the hole will become in your heart." Steve pulled away rather quickly, while this little nudge pulled at his heart.

He felt as if he could not turn away from the life, the girls, the money, the fame, the friends, and the power. He had a sincere problem with appearing weak. He was willing to respect God, but he was not willing to become weak for Him. As he left his mom's house, Steve had an accident that left him clinging to life. He knew deep within his heart that this accident wasn't about him; it was about God's purpose.

As he lay there for months, he was God, alright! Very few people came to visit him. The friends he thought he had never came. The girls who enjoyed spending time with him never came. The money, power, and lifestyle he had were meaningless at this point.

As a ray of hope, one day, a nurse walked into the room and began praying for his recovery. To his chagrin, it was the same woman he had insulted, spat on, poured alcohol on, and had thrown out of the club. Yes, the one he said was not his type! Fortunately, she was the one who had his back. Plus, she was a devout woman of God who did not make it a secret.

Steve had plenty of time to think about what he could not let go of and what he now had to embrace. He had to make a decision:

☐ To live and walk in purpose, *As It Pleased God*.
☐ To die and not live his purpose to please himself.

Steve made a choice three months after the accident. He chose God and the woman who appeared not to be his type. But she was everything he needed and the key to his future.

The decision would have been a no-brainer for me. I could not believe it took Steve that long to decide to do the will of God. However, Steve has totally recovered from his accident, and he has found that *The Psalms Doctor* really works.

As a result of learning how to repent, fast, and pray, there is no turning back for him. Steve is now a well-known minister, married, and has two children. His life has changed in ways he could only have dreamt about. As a matter of fact, He has saved more souls than you would care to imagine, and now, I see why God had to get rid of Steve's distractions.

When we are distracted, it will cause the best of us to jump over the treasure to pick up junk. As a matter of fact, distractions have a way of distorting the value of the people, places, and things we have passed up to fill a temporary void. But make no mistake about it: When all is said and done, the value of the dollar can purchase a lot of things, but character is not one of them.

When we become caught up in the issues of life, we tend to let our guard down in the hope of receiving attention to fill an unrecognizable void. When we fill that void with something other than what we are really missing, we will find ourselves trying to undo things we have already done, doing things we should have left alone from the beginning, or attracting people, places, and things that are out of character for us. Furthermore, it's highly impossible to receive or attract the treasures of life if we have too much junk blocking our way. How can we unblock junk? We must query ourselves, *As It Pleases God*. Here is a list of questions to ask yourself, but not limited to such:

☐ What skills or knowledge do I already have that could be useful in pursuing my goals?

- [ ] What specific goals do I want to achieve, and why are they important to me?
- [ ] What measures can I take right now to start making progress towards my goals?
- [ ] Who can I seek guidance or mentorship from in my desired field?
- [ ] How can I turn my current job or hobbies into opportunities to develop skills relevant to my goals?
- [ ] What are the biggest obstacles standing in the way of my success, and how can I overcome them?
- [ ] What sacrifices am I willing to make in order to achieve my goals?
- [ ] How can I stay motivated and engrossed throughout the process of pursuing my goals?
- [ ] What are some potential setbacks I may face, and how can I prepare for them?
- [ ] How can I continue to learn, grow, and cultivate in my desired field or industry?
- [ ] What are some networking opportunities I can take advantage of to meet others in my desired field?
- [ ] What are some alternative paths or strategies I can pursue if my initial plan doesn't work out?
- [ ] How can I manage my time effectively to balance pursuing my goals with other responsibilities or obligations?
- [ ] What are some specific milestones I can set for myself to track my progress towards my goals?
- [ ] How can I maintain a confident attitude and avoid getting discouraged by setbacks or failures?
- [ ] What are some resources or tools that could be useful in pursuing my goals?
- [ ] How can I leverage my strengths and weaknesses to achieve my goals?

- [ ] What are some potential risks associated with pursuing my goals, and how can I minimize them?
- [ ] What are some examples of others who have achieved similar goals later in life, and how did they do it?
- [ ] What steps can I take today to start moving towards my goals, even if they seem far away?

The above questions are designed to get your wheels turning in the right direction. Why do we need to query ourselves in this manner? Most often, your treasures are right under your nose!

For example, Steve's wife was already presented to him, but He rejected her because she did not appear to be his type. Yet, it was not too late for him; God gave him a second chance.

Remember, you have free will to choose. It's up to you whether or not you take the time or the opportunity to get rid of the junk and sift through the dirt to get to what rightfully belongs to you.

From me to you, your overlooked treasures will always keep their hidden value, whether it's visible to you or not. Once again, it is wise to always approach people, places, and things, *As It Pleases God*, taking ourselves out of the equational efforts. While simultaneously using the Fruits of the Spirit and behaving Christlike. Why? Simply put, Steve could have avoided the accident if he had placed God first, exercised obedience, and treated people right.

We will never know what or who God is using as a footstone, stepping stone, or cornerstone without proper discernment; therefore, it is best to move with Him instead of without Him.

PRAYER

Father, my God, in the Name of Jesus, I am seeking Your face on how to develop trust for myself, with others, and with You. Lord, You know the hurts, pains, and betrayals I have endured in the past that have contributed to my troubled heart. For it is Your power that will bring salvation to my distrustful weariness; therefore, I give this issue to You. I am praying for healing in those areas, as well as healing regarding the environmental conditioning of my thoughts, actions, reactions, words, traumas, biases, and beliefs contributing to my situation.

Father, as I learn how to trust my instincts, as well as those small nudges from within, help me to lean not to my own understanding regarding the ways in which You are going to bless me or direct me. I pray You remove the fear and doubt from within me that would cause me to second-guess Your will or Your way.

My God, I know Your presence is real; I know without You, there would not be me; I know I am a product of my own human nature; I also know there is a time and place for everything under the sun. For this reason, I count myself not to be apprehended because as long as the sun rises in the east and sets in the west every day, as long as there is morning and evening every day, and as long as time does not stop, I know Your divine order is in place, giving me hope for tomorrow. And, according to Your word regarding trust, if I ask for it, believe I have it, and it will be mine. So I lay claim to it right now, in the Name of Jesus, as I overflow with the trustworthy power of the Holy Spirit.

As I exude confidence and peace in my life, I don't want just to say I trust You; I desire for my life, my actions, my reactions, my thoughts, my beliefs, and my conversations to become a representation of my trust in You. Thus giving me the ability to be a living testimony to speak life into the people, places, and things needing what You have to offer. And for this, O' Lord, I give thanks to You, while Your praises continually flow from my lips. Amen.

SCRIPTURE READING:

PSALMS 14
PSALMS 30
PSALMS 45
PSALMS 46
PSALMS 67
PSALMS 135
PSALMS 138

CHAPTER 7

THE PSALMS DOCTOR

In order to embrace "*The Psalms Doctor*," we need to pay attention to what's going on from within us, as well as around us. Our path of mastery is determined by our ability to reach beyond our self-imposed limitations to assume responsibility for our actions, reactions, and the lack thereof.

The Psalms Doctor says that it is easier to blame someone else for our problems, but guess what? It doesn't solve anything. If we take a moment to look back over our lives, we will find the issues we are having right now are the issues we did not pray about, the issues we did not seek God about, or the issues we did not exercise the wisdom that was available to us at that time. Therefore, shifting the blame has become easier, or better yet, emotionally comforting, than taking responsibility for our actions, reactions, or the lack thereof.

The best example I can give regarding *The Psalms Doctor* is to tell Mason's story about an extreme issue with spiritual abuse. Actually, when Mason began to tell me her story, I was in great disbelief until she showed evidence validating her ordeal. What does this mean? She showed me proof with the irrefutable markings.

Here is the story: Mason grew up as a sheltered child who did not realize her weaknesses would expose her to the real world. Nevertheless, Mason knew what type of man she wanted and did not care about voicing her opinion about her likes and dislikes. As destiny would have it, this one particular guy named Eddie took a special liking to Mason. Although she was very cordial, she made it known she wasn't interested by a small gesture of turning up her nose. Well, Eddie was offended by this gesture, which made him determined to make Mason his woman of choice.

Oddly enough, Mason began to take a strange liking to Eddie after many encounters. She thought it was weird, knowing Eddie was not her type. But she blew it off, thinking God was teaching her a lesson about being too picky. As the relationship progressed, her soul was saying he wasn't the one, and the red flags were obvious, but her mind justified her strange behavior.

Mason began to go against everything she believed in. She stopped praying; she stopped reading the Bible; she stopped meditating; she basically stopped everything that kept her spiritually rooted and grounded in God Almighty. Although Mason questioned her actions, she quickly justified them as taking a break from God.

I was confused when Mason made this statement. Then, I quickly interrupted her, asking, 'How can a person want to take a break from God?' She said that she loves God with all her heart, but was overwhelmed with Religion because she was being picked on, bullied, thrown under the bus, and called names by Christians. Then she corrected her statement to say that she wasn't tired of God Himself but overwhelmed by the people proclaiming to serve Him.

As Mason began to fall from grace, if the truth is told, amid her justification efforts, she knew she was taking a downward spiral with this man. For some odd reason, she could not help herself or did not want to.

After months of puppy love, the infatuation began to wear off while reality began to set in. Let Mason tell it; the relationship got boring; Eddie was not her type, and he was out of her league, and he knew it. He felt that he had to keep her spiritually grounded in something, or she would pull away from him. So, he invited her to an event he was hosting, and when they got there, Mason felt out of place.

The people at the event began dancing, spinning around, blowing fire, chanting, etc.; she had no idea she was dating a Houngan (Voodoo Priest). Once she realized who he was, she ran out of the building.

Mason got angry with God because she felt He had let her down. But I was confused when she said God let her down. So, I asked, 'Didn't you stop praying?' 'Did you ask for discernment?' 'Did you even seek God at all?' She explained how naive she became, doing weird things and turning away from God. However, she said that she knew something was off and did not seek God as she should have.

After the event, she was so afraid of him and his practices, but, for some odd reason, she stayed with him. Although she felt stupid for staying, she had no desire to leave him. Mason made it clear she would not partake in his religious practices; however, it did not stop him from trying to draw her in.

After many years of standing her ground on his religious practices, he finally gave up on trying to draw her in. For some reason, she could not find her way back into the arms of God. She could not make that connection until her mom changed the rules of the game.

Mason was still a little naive. Okay, she was very naive; she did not even realize her mom had a crush on her Houngan boyfriend. To add insult to injury, she did not know her mom and boyfriend were secretly having an affair behind her back.

This arrogant, good-for-nothing man began to date the mother in order to keep the daughter bound spiritually. He knew Mason's greatest weakness was her mom.

Every time Mason began to pull away from Eddie, her mom would do something to emotionally traumatize her, and then she would go running back to him for comfort. Like clockwork, Eddie would be waiting for her with open arms to draw her back in again, as she could not see the trees for the forest.

Mason just wanted someone to give her what she could never get from her mother, which was love. She often wondered how the lack of love from her mother could keep her with a man she was not in love with. Once again, she blew it off, not realizing she was spiritually blind to reality due to her weakness.

Even though Mason was going through something with Eddie, she never lost hope. While she wasn't praying like she should, there was an internal knowing that if she did not give up on God or serve another god, He would not give up on her. Somehow, she knew from within the depths of her soul that He would bring her out of that situation one day.

Finally, the scales were removed from her eyes when she and Eddie were engaged in a fun-loving conversation. Then, all of a sudden, her mom calls Eddie's cell phone. Eddie did not tell her that it was her mom calling; however, she knew her mom's voice. As he indulged in the conversation, Mason could hear her mom confiding in Eddie, revealing personal information that should not be discussed with her boyfriend.

As Mason listened to the ultimate betrayal, her mom made a powerhouse statement, opening her eyes. She said, "My daughter hates me because she thinks I am in love with you." Mason dropped her head and began to cry. She knew at that moment that her mom wanted Eddie for herself, and something was not right about their relationship.

Eddie cut the conversation short with her mom as Mason fell apart emotionally before his very eyes. Riddled with pain, she cried all night long. She knew her mom was treacherous when it came down to a man.

As a child, she saw her mom cheat with her best friend's husband, she saw her mom cheat with her dad's close friends, and she saw her mom cheat with co-workers. Honestly, she never thought her mom would cheat with her child's boyfriend. Wow, what would provoke a woman to cheat with her own child's man? Is it money? Is it sex? Is it envy? Is it greed? Is it control? Or is it just trifling? Who knows, but her conscience will soon become her guide!

As time went on, Mason began to watch and pray about her situation while drifting away from Eddie emotionally. Then, she began to drift away mentally. And once she escaped the mental enslavement, she was able to see how Eddie controlled her, she was able to see how he was cheating on her, she was able to see how he was using her, she was able to see how he manipulated her, she was able to see how he tried to keep her from reading the Bible, and she was able to see how he became her mom's personal maintenance man right under her nose.

Unfortunately, this was only the beginning of Mason's torture! Eddie realized he was losing his grip on her. The more he began to perform rituals to control her, the more she prayed for God to release her. This woman was indeed in a real spiritual battle! Now, this is what I would call sleeping with the enemy. Mason had some real issues at this point; nevertheless, she was willing to fight for her freedom because Eddie crossed the line when he started fooling around with her mother.

As fate would have it, I ran into Mason at a church gathering; she explained her situation to me and asked me to pray with her about it. In the middle of our prayer, Mason began to vomit to no avail. I explained to her that God was trying to purge her from the situation she was in. I also told her to stop having sex with that man, especially if she wanted to break free.

As *The Psalms Doctor*, I told her that once God gets her out of this situation, she must never look back. No matter what happens, she must stand her ground. I gave her a prayer to read every day, and I explained to her how to use the Power of Psalms to help her with her spiritual battle.

A few months rolled by, and she became on fire for God again. Yet, she had to live with Eddie mocking her about how weak her God was. He also stated she needed something stronger than the Bible to shake him off. Nevertheless, Mason kept praying and reading her Bible.

Then all of a sudden, out of nowhere, her life began to change for the better. She moves out, eager to move on with her life, and here comes Eddie, trying to rope her back in again. She was tempted, but she remembered our conversation about not looking back.

The more she pulled away from Eddie, the more desperate he became. He began to pull out little tricks to shake her emotionally, but it did not work. He tried little stunts to shake her mentally; it did not work. He started damaging her property; it did not work. He tried to sift her spiritually, but it did not work. He was at a loss; he finally realized God was indeed more powerful than he was.

So, he decided to let go of Mason; however, in doing so, he needed someone to blame. So he decided to make Mason's mom pay for what she caused with that one inappropriate, untimely phone call. When they say karma is no joke, they mean it! Out of revenge, Eddie decides to drive Mason's mom crazy with one of his rituals as compensation for the pain he has to endure for losing the one woman he truly loved.

Mason learned the power of prayer in conjunction with reading applicable scriptures from the Book of Psalms; as a result, she finally has peace in her life. Her faith in God is unshakeable after that ordeal with Eddie. She is now married to a wonderful man who believes in God Almighty and who really loves her for who she is. Eddie is still running from woman to woman, looking for Mason inside of each one of them. Mason's mom is still mentally unstable and refuses to admit to any of her wrongdoings.

How do we break soul ties? There are many ways to break them; however, we must place God first, *As It Pleases Him*, use the Fruits of the Spirit, and behave Christlike. There is no need to be rude, hateful, or difficult; nonetheless, here are a few ways to break them, but not limited to such:

☐ Identify the toxic relationship: To break soul ties, you must first identify the toxic relationship and acknowledge that it is harmful to your emotional and mental health.

☐ Create distance: Once you have identified the toxic relationship, create distance between yourself and the person. This could involve limiting communication, avoiding physical contact, or even cutting off all contact.

☐ Focus on your well-being: Prioritize your emotional and mental well-being by engaging in activities that make you happy and fulfilled.

☐ Seek support: Reach out to friends, family, or a therapist for support as you work towards breaking the soul tie.

☐ Cut off all communication: Sever all communication with the person can be an effective way to break the soul tie.

☐ Release negative emotions: Identify and release any negative emotions you have towards the person. This could involve talking to a trusted friend or therapist, or even writing down your feelings in a journal.

☐ Practice forgiveness: Forgiving the person can help release the emotional attachment and allow you to move forward.

☐ Focus on personal growth: Invest in personal growth by engaging in activities that help you become a better version of yourself.

☐ Create new experiences: Move on with your life, doing new things without involving the severed soul tie, such as trying a new hobby or visiting a new place.

☐ Exercise self-care: Nurture yourself physically, emotionally, and mentally by doing things that make you feel good.

☐ Avoid triggers: Dodge situations that may trigger memories or emotions associated with the person.

☐ Seek spiritual guidance: Seek guidance from a spiritual leader, pastor, or counselor who can help you find peace and healing.

☐ Take time to heal: Give yourself time to heal and process your emotions.

☐ Set boundaries: Establish healthy restrictions with the person to prevent any further emotional entanglement.

☐ Let go of expectations: Absolve any expectations you may have had for the relationship or the person.

☐ Practice patience: Breaking a soul tie takes time and patience, so be kind to yourself and take it one day at a time.

☐ Find closure: Seek closure by expressing your feelings or saying goodbye to the person (even if it's just mentally).

☐ Avoid self-blame: Avoid blaming yourself for the situation or for any mistakes you may have made.

☐ Focus on the future: Focus on creating a positive future for yourself and let go of any negative emotions or attachments from the past.

PRAYER

Father, my God, in the Name of Jesus, today I break the ties binding me. With the Blood of the Lamb, I also cut every cord, trying to control me secretly.

I renounce all ill will or the violation of my free will, causing me to become a puppet on a string. I command my Warring Angels to destroy anything that's not conducive to my well-being or the will that You have set for my life. From this point on, no ground can hold the ties that bind my soul without my permission, in the Name of Jesus.

I confess and repent that I have been mentally, physically, emotionally, and spiritually connected to someone in a way that is not pleasing to You. I declare that any negative influence through sexual immorality, emotional manipulation, spiritual deception, or any other means or adverse influences this person has had on me is broken, and any adverse influence I have had on them is broken as well. Restore my soul and fill me with Your Holy Spirit. I thank you for setting me free from every soul tie hindering me from fulfilling your purpose. I claim back my identity, my destiny, and my authority in Christ Jesus. Amen.

SCRIPTURE READING:

PSALMS 31
PSALMS 36
PSALMS 91

CHAPTER 8

GET OUT OF YOUR OWN WAY

Are you blocked? Are you overwhelmed with obstacles? Do your thoughts or beliefs hold you back? Do you fear taking risks? Are you wallowing in a bed of doubt? According to the Heavenly of Heavens, it is time to *Get Out Of Your Own Way*.

Can we really block ourselves? Absolutely! It happens all too often, especially for those who fail to listen, learn, and grow. *Getting Out Of Your Own Way* is crucial to achieving success, joy, happiness, and peace, *As It Pleases God*. Often, we are our own biggest obstacle, whether it's due to limiting beliefs, self-doubt, fear, perception, or old habits. However, our perception plays a crucial role in doing so.

Regardless of who we are, why we are, or what we possess, we can't get away from our perception. When we walk, our perception is there. When we talk, our perception is there. When we think, our perception is there. When we take action, our perception is there. No matter what we do, our perception has a way of tracking us down like our shadow. With the proper reflection of light, our perceptional shadow will appear. When it makes an appearance, we need to be adequately equipped, *As It Pleases God.*

My best example of perception is from this con artist, Tiffany. When I met her, she was a little capricious, but she had a way with people. She could get any type of information that she wanted by playing dumb. She often cracked jokes about prying into the lives of others; actually, getting the dirt on people was her favorite pastime.

Prying and snooping were her thing, and she knew it. Tiffany would steal the identity of someone right under their nose. She started with her family members and then graduated to anyone she could benefit from. As Tiffany lived up to her reputation, this woman was not to be trusted with anything or anyone. I was a little leery when she shared her story, but I knew the Blood of Jesus covered me to get this story for the Kingdom of God.

Although Tiffany pretended to be an airhead, she kept a file on everyone. If she knew their name, she had a file on them. She documented everything, including her sexual partners and their types of activities. Tiffany believed everyone had something to hide, and it was her God-given duty to uncover it while doing her best to keep her own life private and under lock and key.

As I got to know Tiffany a little better, I realized Tiffany had dark skeletons she really needed to keep hidden. This lady had secrets that would put her and others under the jailhouse. Nevertheless, this is what she shared with me.

As a child, she began seducing her uncle for lunch money and enough money to buy her friends as well. The more she did it, the easier it became, and the more she enjoyed it. She continued for years until she got bored, needing more than just lunch money.

As a hustling youngster, she decided to step up her game; however, her game plan was not a plan of an average child. I could not believe that after she had blackmailed her uncle enough, she decided to seduce her mom and her sister's boyfriends for money. Tiffany perceived her mom and sister as being too fat and ugly to please their man, so she decided to please them for money and a ticket out of the ghetto. Did it work? Absolutely.

Tiffany moved on with her life and her secrets. She no longer had to live in a roach-infested house, nor did she have to deal with the guilt of what she was doing. With her newfound fancy-free lifestyle, she was free to do what she wanted, when she wanted, and how she wanted while preying on the weaknesses of men.

She perceived men to be weak for pretty women, especially if they were married, lonely, and bored. She said she would find her victims by befriending their wives. Tiffany would find out the weaknesses of a person's home by having the wife confide in her, and then she would track down the husband to befriend him. This slick chick would find out all of his dirt and record their phone calls to blackmail him into having an affair.

Of course, Tiffany's manipulative schemes did not work all the time, but she had a good success rate in getting what she wanted. On the other hand, if she did not, she would go to her big file cabinet. Tiffany would pull out her ammunition to create confusion, spreading all of their dirt to break up their home.

There was no doubt about it; Tiffany was ruthless! This woman knew the rules of the game, and she wasn't ashamed to flaunt her confidence. But here is the kicker that tickled me: Tiffany would not bring a woman around her man PERIOD! She did not care if it was her mom, sister, relative, or friend—nobody came to her house, and she would not take her man to another woman's house.

While Tiffany's perceptional conscience became her ultimate guide, she did not trust a woman at all. For good reasons, she did not have many friends. In my opinion, this was her way of subconsciously protecting herself from being hurt, losing her man to another woman, or offsetting dirty deeds. Unfortunately, she perceived all women to be like her.

As she told me this story, I could only think about this one scripture, "*So as a man thinketh in his heart, so is he.*" She was actually trying to protect herself from becoming a victim of her own schemes; therefore, she could never get out of her own way. As a result, she created her environment based totally on her perception of how she viewed herself, as well as her past, which eventually gave birth to her reality.

As Tiffany became a little older and wiser, she decided to settle down after meeting Wallace. He was an intelligent, retired military man who had been around the world and back again. He firmly believes that there is nothing new under the sun. So Tiffany's little mind games did not faze him at all.

Wallace, the newfound boo, set booby traps for Tiffany. He perceived she would snoop through his things like a typical woman. The more she snooped, the more he played with her mind. Tiffany's little snooping games began to backfire on her mentally and emotionally. Even though she did not confront him about what she was finding, her conversations began to give her away. Wallace knew he had to teach her a lesson for violating his privacy and the privacy of others.

A few months later, Wallace went out of town to get away. Tiffany stayed up all night trying to dig up dirt on him to figure out where he was going or who he was going with, and she found nothing. The elements of not knowing or not finding anything began to drive her insane. So the master snooper gathered up enough courage to break into his house with a key she duplicated a couple of months back. Tiffany was not the least bit nervous; she walked into his house as if she lived there. She began rummaging through his things, looking for anything she could use against him.

All of a sudden, Wallace puts a gun to her head. He stopped her dead in her tracks. He said, "I should blow your brains out." She began to tremble and cry, pleading for her life. Wallace was so angry that she came into his house without his permission that he almost choked the life out of her. He knew he had to get rid of her because she was too comfortable violating his privacy, especially not being his wife.

This incident would have caused a normal person to stop snooping, but not Tiffany. After they had broken up, Tiffany continued to dig up dirt on him without his knowledge to use it against him one day. As she moved on to her next victim, this is where all of her deeds came back to bite her in the butt.

Tiffany wanted this new guy named Ben. It did not matter what she had to do, who she had to hurt, or what information she had to dig up; she had to have him. Six months into pursuing this man, Tiffany broke up this man's relationship with his baby's mother, resulting in them (his former girlfriend and child) living in a shelter for weeks.

Two months later, she moved into his house, taking over everything as if Ben had married her. This time, Tiffany thought she had met the man of her dreams. He promised her the world, and she fell for it. He took her on trips; they went out on the town every weekend, and they just could not get enough of each other.

A year later, something changed. The man of her dreams started to become her worst nightmare. She had met a straight-up womanizing alcoholic who was on the down-low. As long as he was getting what he wanted, he did not care about anything else, and she did not realize this until she was head-over-heels in love with him. For some odd reason, she could not let him go or risk being embarrassed by another failed relationship. As he began to slip through her fingers, she tried to buy his love, and it did work for a few hours—then he was back to his old self again.

Tiffany was at a loss with this guy; she tried using information against him, but it did not work. He did not care about anything; he had nothing to lose, and he couldn't care less about what people thought of him. Tiffany's little blackmail schemes did not work with him as he began to drive her crazy, especially when she found homemade pornographic movies of him having sex with overweight women and men.

It seemed as if Tiffany had a problem with overweight women. She could not believe a man would engage in an intimate relationship with a heavy woman. Not only that, but she could not believe he would enjoy having sex with a man as well. These are the two contributing factors that drove her crazy or, better yet, suicidal.

As Ben began to find out the truth about Tiffany, he lost all respect for her. He did not realize he had brought a conniving, blackmailing, backbiting woman into his house. Ben could not stand the sight of her, so he avoided her as much as possible. The more he stayed away, the more unstable she became, making herself sick just to get his attention.

Tiffany went to the extreme of getting pregnant, which was a bad idea on her behalf. Ben went absolutely crazy because he did not want another child, especially from a mentally unstable woman who concocted a scheme, causing him to put his own child on the streets. He felt as if she was trying to trap him, and he was not going to allow that to happen again. He threatened to sabotage her lawsuit if she did not have an abortion, so she did.

Unfortunately, the willful loss of Tiffany's child was the straw that broke the camel's back. Being that she chose money over her unborn child, she began to mix alcohol with her medication, trying to commit suicide. Ben did not care; he wanted her out of his house, and he would not even take her to the hospital because of her stupidity. Amazingly, she had to call the ambulance for her own suicide attempt.

For some odd reason, Tiffany refused to leave this man's house. She used every trick in the book to stay, but Ben had one trick up his sleeve that would drive her away, and that was another woman. He began to bring other women to the house, and he did not extend any form of respect for her; eventually, she left with her tail between her legs, holding on to the memories of what would never be.

The act of being observant is one thing, but plain old snooping is another. The violation of privacy is abusive, and there is no excuse for snooping without permission with a person who is of age.

Regardless of where we are in life, we must do our homework on the people, places, and things in our lives. Yes, we must get the facts; however, it's not necessary to violate the privacy of anyone or snoop. Simply ask fact-finding questions. And yes, I do agree we must know who or what we are dealing with, and we must also know who or what we will not deal with. Living by this principle will help us not to settle for people, places, and things we cannot or choose not to deal with.

Our best bet is to get all the details or information before we commit to a person, place, thing, or event. However, if we have to violate the privacy of someone or create an abusive situation to get it, then more than likely, that's not ideal.

As for snooping Tiffany, she moved on with her life, but her health began to fail dramatically due to the extended use and abuse of her pain medications and sleeping pills. Not only that, she now has an incurable STD she got from Ben, and can no longer have unprotected sex with another man.

To add insult to injury, she has been diagnosed as a paranoid schizophrenic. She thinks everyone is out to get her. She is constantly paranoid about someone watching her, tapping her phone, or getting her personal information. Tiffany never realized her snooping would become her ultimate downfall. Sadly, she is now in a mental institution where she's able to receive help for her condition, because she refused to use *The Psalms Doctor* to help her through her situation.

Does our perception really create our reality? The answer is no; however, it does INFLUENCE it. We create our reality with our self-talk, our ability to refocus, our thinking, and *Getting Out Of Our Own Way*. Our perception is used as a tool to positively or negatively INFLUENCE our thoughts, actions, reactions, words, and demeanor. Therefore, if we use our perception as a positive tool of understanding to become better, stronger, and wiser, we will find that our perception will begin to work for us and not against us.

In order to survive in the real world and *Get Out Of Your Own Way*, there are two things we must possess: RESPECT and DISCIPLINE. We will find our unparalleled sacrifices are usually made in the areas in which we lack discipline or the areas in which we lack respect. Therefore, if we approach life, *As It Pleases God*, not pleasing ourselves, our lives will take on a whole new trajectory without having to scheme, get over, manipulate, snoop, or player hate. Here is a list to fine-tune our perception, but not limited to such:

☐ Practice mindfulness, doing things *As It Pleases God*.
☐ Be fully present and prayerful.
☐ Engage in meditation with positive affirmations.
☐ Calm your mind, think, and observe.
☐ Challenge your assumptions, biases, and perspectives.
☐ Surround yourself with diverse people and ideas.
☐ Take time to reflect on your thoughts and emotions.
☐ Read books and articles from different authors and viewpoints, including the Bible.
☐ Ask questions and actively listen to others.
☐ Learn a new skill or hobby to expand your knowledge.
☐ Practice empathy by imagining yourself in someone else's shoes.
☐ Use visualization techniques to enhance your creativity and problem-solving abilities.
☐ Spend more time in nature.
☐ Keep a gratitude journal to focus on the positive aspects of life.
☐ Set goals and work towards achieving them.
☐ Embrace failure as an opportunity to learn and grow.
☐ Practice self-compassion, helpfulness, and kindness.
☐ Use the Fruits of the Spirit and behave Christlike.
☐ Seek out feedback and constructive criticism.

Getting Out Of Your Own Way is easier now. Use the checklist with *The Psalms Doctor*, and nothing can hold you back.

PRAYER

My Father, which art in Heaven, in the Mighty Name of Jesus, I am seeking Divine Direction. Please do not allow me to fall by the wayside due to my perception. You know the way I should go or to avoid, so I trust You to go before me and stand behind me in all I do, say, and become, *As It Pleases You.*

O'Lord, grant me the wisdom and clarity to perceive things correctly. Please help me to see things as they truly are and not as I wish them to be. Guide my thoughts and actions so I may always act with integrity, making decisions that are just and fair. Give me the strength to resist the temptation to judge others unfairly or to make assumptions without all the facts. May I always strive to be open-minded, compassionate, and understanding. Teach me to listen to others with empathy and to seek to understand their perspective. Father, help me to see the good in people and situations, even when things are difficult. Thanks for Your guidance and blessings. May I always walk in Your light, truth, and mercy that will draw them unto You, as *I Get Out Of My Own Way.* In Jesus' Name, I pray. Amen.

SCRIPTURE READING:

PSALMS 7
PSALMS 10
PSALMS 12
PSALMS 40
PSALMS 51

CHAPTER 9

THE MONOPOLY

We have tons of books on the market telling us how to master the game of love, how to do this, and how to do that, but let me say this: There is a difference between playing games, following the rules, and exercising common sense. In the Eye of God, tit-for-tat games will cause us to play ourselves short in the end due to the loss of credibility or reliability.

Once our credibility is lost, it is hard to regain, especially when we are exchanging lies and half-truths. Besides, the last thing we would ever want to do is to have someone give up on us because we are playing too many games or have them stop believing in us due to unreliability.

The Psalms Doctor says the game of love is such a delicate game that we should not run the risk of playing with someone's feelings. Why? It leaves room for someone to get hurt, and hurting someone out of mere selfishness will cause this game to eventually backfire. It may not come back at that moment, but the Law of Reciprocity is in full effect; therefore, one must tread very carefully when classifying oneself as a PLAYER.

As the cycle of life has it, the games we play will eventually play out! Plus, there is someone out there who can play our game better than us can and win at it. Therefore, it is better to play by the rules, such as Godly principles and the Fruits of the Spirit, to ensure one stays on the winning end of the spectrum, even if it appears as if they are on the losing end.

There are times when it's the CHASE that gets a woman or a man into a relationship. We do not want someone who is such an EASY catch that anyone can get! During the chase, some of us use game playing as our point of leverage to get a particular individual of interest. But I must say that if we are going to play games to get someone, we must have enough game to keep them. In my opinion, we can get into as many relationships as we so desire, but if we are not able to keep a relationship together after the catch, then what? Now the question is, "What do we do when the game is over, and our catch is now on our backs, driving us crazy?" Do we move on to another game? Do we continue the same cycle? Or, do we learn how to tighten up our game?

When we start playing games in a relationship, we will soon find that there is an onset of increased arguments. In the game of life, we all have a desire to win; however, in a relationship, when games are being played, the rules change on a moment-by-moment basis depending on who is winning and who is getting hurt. When this begins to happen, we will find that we will begin to feel like enemies battling for territories of the heart. Incidentally, waiting for the next punch line or who is going to win at a particular game, the couple then ceases to enjoy the relationship or each other.

When we have to stay on guard with our emotions with someone we are trying to trust with our hearts, it is not a comfortable feeling. Actually, it leaves room for trust issues to surface and interests to change with time. This is a level of immaturity that will eventually cause some sort of defeat or sabotage. If not now, give it some time; the game will backfire because when we become opponents in a relationship, we do not fight fairly! In my opinion, this is the deal breaker in a relationship, and due to this downfall or breakdown, it is best to part ways before continuing on this path of destruction.

Why must we sever opponent relationships? If this type of relationship is continued, the arguments will increase, especially about power, money, sex, the children...you name it, it will happen. Please make no mistake about it: arguing with our partner or spouse is not a reason to part ways. But having arguments due to constantly playing opponent mind games with our partner, resulting in harbored bitterness, anger, revenge, or rage, should raise red flags. In addition, if it has led up to some form of abuse, it is definitely a reason to draw a line in the sand on that relationship unless one changes their behavior.

Monopolizing Truth

Spiritual monopoly has been around since the beginning of time, and it's not going anywhere anytime soon. For this reason, in all honesty, everyone has their price, which leads me to the question, "Is there a prostitute in every woman and man?" Most would say no, but I say YES. If you are adamant about not having an inner prostitute, then there is definitely a pimp from within. Let me explain: There is temptation in everyone, whether we admit it or not.

We are conditioned to think all prostitutes are on the street corners or in the strip clubs; however, I beg to differ. There are unregulated pimps and prostitutes all around us. Actually, the best pimps and prostitutes are not on the streets. They live among us, next door to us, and sometimes within us. Am I calling you a prostitute or a pimp? No. I am not calling anyone a prostitute or pimp. I am only bringing about awareness from within.

In the Eye of God, whether we are the prostituter, prostitutee, pimper, or pimpee, our human nature causes us to gravitate to the men and women who possess money, power, or fame. On the other hand, we often stray away from those who have little or nothing to offer, with zero benefits from our perspective. Misgoverned monopolies from within cause seven things to happen, but not limited to such:

- ☐ Spiritual, mental, emotional, physical, and financial prostitution.
- ☐ Pride of Life.
- ☐ Gold Digging.
- ☐ Brown Nosing.
- ☐ Using sex as leverage in a relationship.
- ☐ Buying your way through life.
- ☐ Manipulation and Control of the weak by mental, physical, emotional, spiritual, or financial enslavement.

Are these not all forms of prostitution? Wherever you find idolatry, you will find prostitution! Of course, we would not use the word prostitution because it's not a politically correct word to use when we are selling our souls in exchange for material and personal gain. We experience it on the job, where most of the mental prostitution and brown-nosing takes place. We experience it in the church, where spiritual prostitution is at its best. We experience it in our relationships and in our homes, where the gold-digging or sexual leverage takes place. IT IS EVERYWHERE, but not limited to these certain places!

At a very young age, I had a deep infatuation with fancy, sporty cars. My father would always say to me, "Do not go crazy over fancy cars because you do not know what they had to do to get them." As a child, I did not grasp the true meaning of what he was saying. Now, as an adult with a bit of experience under my belt, I understand. Some go about getting what they want the right way, and some get things the wrong way; who am I to judge, right? Although everyone has done something they are not proud of at some point. Still, it does not exempt us from exercising practical wisdom.

In order to find out about the pimping prostitute from within, just honestly ask yourself two questions:

- ☐ Can I truly be happy with who I am WITHOUT money, power, or sex?
- ☐ Can I truly be happy with who I am WITH money, power, or sex?

The first question creates the prostitute from within, and the second question creates the pimp from within. If left unchecked, lack creates desperation, igniting the prostituting spirit, and over-abundance creates arrogance, igniting the pimping spirit. Is it the same for everyone? Yes. We will all have thoughts, but we will not all ACT UPON the thoughts or the temptations of the prostituting or pimping spirit. Those who proclaim to be a saint without negative insinuations flowing through the mind are liars!

How can I call someone a liar? I come as the appointed *Psalms Doctor*, so I am not here to sugarcoat the truth. If this happened in the Garden of Eden, what makes us any different? We are no different; therefore, negative seedling thoughts will come and go.

Unfortunately, it is the LIES we tell ourselves that cause us to get got, bringing shame or a cover-up. On the other hand, the truth eliminates cover-up or shame. We do not need to tell the world our business or details, but when dealing with negative thoughts, emotions, and desires, we must come clean to God Almighty. If not, the seed will continue to grow. Why? It is not regrafted or pruned, *As It Pleases God*.

For example, with all due respect, we have the pastor's children becoming the most rebellious. Why? Once again, it is the lies. Knowing the inside truths while witnessing the lies creates distrust in the household. When they have the same opportunity to teach them how to reverse the negative into a positive, turn bad into good, and how to right a wrong. Instead, they condition their children to trust the lie more than the truth. So, they rebel by default due to masks, pretense, and playing with the Word of God while the negative seed continues to germinate.

Does this happen to worldly families? Absolutely. But the ratio of rebellion is astounding compared to Believers and unbelievers, especially when it comes down to good fruits vs. rotten fruits. When unbelievers use the Fruits of the Spirit by default while Believers know nothing about them at all, something is definitely wrong!

Thoughts come and go; it is what we hold on to positively or negatively that makes the difference, *As It Pleases God* or as it pleases ourselves. Here is the deal: Believer or not, the pimp or prostitute from within does not make it to reality until we act upon our thoughts. Yes, when we take action, it changes the rules of the game. The more we indulge positively or negatively, the easier it becomes until it is second nature.

Materialism at Its Finest

Materialism has become a plague. When a person enters into a relationship for personal gain, they are considered a gold digger. It's time out for pretending! For example: What do you call a wife who withholds sex because her husband quit his job, forgot her birthday, or took her to McDonald's for their anniversary? An angry wife, right? If the truth were to be told, love runs out real quick when our money starts to look funny, right? We do not want to hear about our motives for silent prostitution because reality hurts.

A person with a gold-digging mentality is nothing more than a prostitute on the down low, and a Sugar Daddy or Sugar Momma is nothing more than a pimp on the down low. Men are taking care of women, and women (Cougars) are taking care of men. What about the innocent individuals who have a desire for true love? Is it a thing of the past? Maybe or maybe not!

To my amazement, I have found that we have just as many gold-digging males as we do females. Everyone wants something, whether we admit it or not. This type of *Monopoly* may include financial support, emotional support, a do-boy, a slave, a side chick, and the list goes on. We have our own reasons, wants, and desires for why we do what we do, and do not do what we need to do.

Let me clear this up; there is nothing wrong with being concerned about your own financial security; however, a gold digger's ultimate goal is financial security from someone other than oneself. They use fake emotions to gain the trust of their victims and then use them for material gain. This epidemic of material gain has caused countless divorces and breakups due to the loss of a job or business. The marriage vow, "For better or for worse," does not mean a thing to a gold digger. They are in the relationship only for the money; when it's gone, they are too. If we are asking or being asked these questions like:

- ☐ Where do you live?
- ☐ Do you own your home?
- ☐ What do you do for a living?
- ☐ How much do you make a year?
- ☐ How many children do you have?

These are questions to determine our net worth or the type of lifestyle that we are accustomed to. These are also the questions that provoke the prostitute or pimp from within.

In order to see if a person is interested in you, delay answering these types of questions. Instead, tell them about you as an individual and the things you like to do. If they are interested, they will ask questions to find out more about you as a person. If they do not, you will automatically know they are only interested in you for the money or sex.

The less you tell a gold digger, the easier it becomes to weed them out. You must take a little time to observe their behavior and conversations. However, if your goal is to be a "Sugar Daddy or Sugar Momma," then this does not apply to you, but if you are looking for someone to love you for you, then keep reading.

Regardless of the thoughts we voice, our actions speak loudly, even if we mask them with seeming perfection. While divorce can result from a variety of complex factors, some common reasons why people divorce include, but are not limited to such:

- [ ] Communication problems.
- [ ] Infidelity.
- [ ] Betrayal.
- [ ] Financial issues.
- [ ] Disagreements about parenting styles.
- [ ] Differences in values or lifestyle choices.
- [ ] Substance abuse.
- [ ] Mental health issues.
- [ ] Physical or emotional abuse.

More importantly, if they want us to stay out of their business, they will say irreconcilable differences. If the communication is not there, flee. And if you feel as if a person is only around you for the money, flee. If not, you will set yourself up to become a statistic. How to spot a user or gold digger:

- [ ] They cannot keep a job.
- [ ] Everything is always someone else's fault.
- [ ] They only call you when they need something.
- [ ] They will always talk about themselves.
- [ ] Their conversation changes when they need something. (baby talk, sexy talk, etc.)
- [ ] They are very materialistic.
- [ ] They have a champagne taste on a beer budget.

- [ ] They get angry when they do not receive a gift from you.
- [ ] They only have sex with you when you buy them something.
- [ ] They make you pay for everything and never buy you anything.

When the key to a person's heart is through money, is there a difference between people who exchange sex for money? The answer is "NO." There is no difference.

Be True to Thyself
When it comes down to telling the truth about the prostitute or pimp from within, we will find we tend to shy away from being honest with ourselves. Here is one young lady named Megan who knows about this all too well. Her story moved me to write this chapter, holding nothing back about the truth we need to face, *As It Pleases God.*

Here is the story: Respect and discipline were instilled in Megan at a very young age, and she was proud to be a very respectful and polite woman with certain values and standards. However, Megan had a few flaws, which caused her to become insecure. She was able to hide her insecurities most of the time by staying to herself and minding her business. Although she was a brilliant little girl, her flaws made her feel inferior to those who appeared not to have any flaws at all.

Her first step of discipline came when she started reading the Bible every day. She did not become self-confident overnight, but her discipline paid off quite well. Today, this woman is so well-spoken; it's unbelievable how her respect and discipline enabled her to top the charts with her written and spoken words of wisdom. However, along with her wisdom came her most significant test with POWER, MONEY, AND SEX.

Megan hit a fork in the road with her business. It began to fail while she did almost everything to keep it afloat. The economy put her in a position where she began to lose money. She had excellent ideas, a great plan, great marketing, great everything, but no money to finance it. The economy put Megan between a rock and a hard place. She could not believe God would bless her so much, only to lose it.

As Megan began to change gears to keep her business running, she would encounter a lot of people who were willing to help her, but there was a catch. They wanted something that violated Megan's will. They had a bargaining tool that made it very tempting for her, but not feasible in the Eye of God.

Nevertheless, this one guy named Luke offered to bring her out of the hole with her business if she became his woman. He appeared to be genuinely concerned about her well-being; therefore, she thought about it and said, "That's not a bad deal because he seems nice." So she began to go out with him.

On the 3rd date, he began to touch her in a way that made her feel uncomfortable, violating her integrity. As she began to move away, he began to push her head down between his legs. Megan resisted, but she could not believe she had let her guard down only to become Luke's next freak for the sake of helping with her business.

So she spoke up, saying, "I am not your prostitute!" He said, "You need something, and I need something, so we are even. Give me what I want, and I'll give you what you want."

The smirk on his face instantly turned Megan off; therefore, she ended the date, jumped into her car, and went home. She realized at that point that he only wanted sex from her and not to really help her. Luke called her for months; she would not take his call. She thought he was disgusting, and she wasn't willing to lose her soul to have him save her business. She would rather lose everything than give Luke the satisfaction of saying she had to prostitute herself for something God has blessed her with.

Megan lost all of her friends during this time of drought; no one came around, and no one offered her any help. She was all alone, questioning God. As money got really low for Megan, she was short a few dollars on her light bill; she asked a long-lost friend of hers for help, but he just gave her the run-around. When she finally caught up with him, he asked her, "What are you going to give me if I help you?" She said, "I will pay you back!" He said, "That's not what I want." She said, "I am not giving it up; I would rather sit in the dark before I allow you to violate my integrity." He said, "Okay, sit in the dark. You will be back."

Megan could not believe her long-time friend wanted to break her down, especially in her time of need. Although God made a way for her, she cried all night long. Her heart wasn't broken because she didn't have the money to pay the light bill. Her heart was broken because, in her time of weakness and vulnerability, her friend tried to take advantage of her and the situation to bring shame to her name, ruining her credibility and relevancy.

Megan did not settle for the sexual, economic, or emotional abuse that was placed before her. She was determined to use *The Psalms Doctor* to find her way into greatness, *As It Pleased God*. As a result, Megan eliminated all of the so-called friends who mistreated or used her during her time of famine. She did not lose her company; actually, her integrity saved it! Her company became a multi-million dollar empire. Megan learned that insecurities are designed to drive greatness out of us, regardless of how it may seem at the time.

Insecurity is basically an obstruction or hindrance that creates a superficial image of weakness. When a weakness is exposed to others, most often, we retreat out of shame instead of taking our weakness and turning it into something great.

An exposed weakness is better than a covered weakness; as a matter of fact, an exposed weakness will give us more of an incentive to work on that area. But on the other hand, when our weakness is covered up, it is easier to overlook or make excuses for it. The truth is, we all have some form of an impediment. Some are able to cover them up better than others, but in reality, we all fall short in some areas of our lives! However, this is not the time to worry about falling short or being perfect!

For this reason, Megan understands that there is cause and effect all around us. However, when we try to change the rules of the game by fighting the effect and not the cause, then we can pretty much expect disarray and disorder to take place in our lives. When we become selfish about having things our way, we will find we limit the way in which we are able to excel, especially when the feeling of negative déjà vu is involved.

When déjà vu presents itself in your life, that's your cue to embrace the opportunity to do things better by enhancing what you are not doing or curtailing what you are doing. Finding the cause of something can and will give you better leverage over the effects in your life. Just remember, an impediment cannot keep you blocked if you look for the benefit. When you do that, greatness is inevitable, creating an open door of opportunity for you to take advantage of.

Today, take a look at the timeline of your life to see what's repeating itself and why. The image we hold of ourselves will determine whether we are going to become a survivor or prey.

Megan enabled herself to become faithfully and meekly interdependent, allowing everyone to play their role in her life. She mysteriously found that when nothing else seemed to work, her faithful interdependence with her Heavenly Father would!

It was through her faith and humility that she attracted that one idea, thought, reaction, or whatever, changing her life forever. Megan is a true survivor, and she teaches others to embrace their true value as well. Megan's trust handed her a humility that people could not understand; actually, this woman has a way of humbling herself to elevate others into divine greatness. She does not pretend to be better than anyone else; she makes it her business to present herself like a humble child to find the diamonds in the rough. She understood that if she appreciated life, it would make her survival a little easier. She said that the best way to survive a situation or circumstance in life is to appreciate it and become grateful for every experience.

I must agree with Megan; money can buy most of what we want, but it cannot always buy what we need. When I was on my deathbed several years ago, I was the youngest person in the Intensive Care Unit. The doctors said I was in bad shape, but I knew I was in that unit for a reason. So I decided to talk with the older men and women there, asking them one important question: "If you could rewrite your life, what would you do differently?" They all said, "Spend more time with my family." I never heard anyone speak about money, a job, or material wealth; they only spoke about family. I thought it was so amazing to spend years attaining wealth, and then in their last years, they wished they could have enjoyed the one thing they had neglected. Above all, our spiritual development is imperative to conquer the temptations that are designed to sift us.

PRAYER

My Father, which art in Heaven, it is You I worship, resisting the proud, giving grace to the humble. Please grant me the virtue of true humility, of which Your Son showed us an example by His words and deeds. Deliver and cover me, O Lord, from the pride of my heart, which hinders Your grace from entering my soul. Teach me to esteem myself *As It Pleases You*, without having to create a bed of lies, masks, and secret skeletons waiting to emerge to bring shame to my name or the Kingdom.

As I invoke the Holy Spirit for guidance, Lord, I thank You for all the blessings You have given me and for Your constant presence in my life. I confess that sometimes I struggle to trust You and Your plans. And, I sometimes worry about the future and doubt Your goodness. For this, I repent, asking You to forgive me for my lack of faith and to fill me with Your peace, confidence, and joy.

Help me to trust You more each day, to surrender my worries and fears to You, and to rest in Your promises. You are my rock, my refuge, and my hope. You are the SOURCE of all wisdom, power, glory, and grace. You are the only one who can satisfy my deepest needs and desires as I place my flesh under the subjection of the Holy Spirit.

Lord, I choose to trust the truth, *As It Pleases You*. In the Name of Jesus. Amen.

SCRIPTURE READING:

PSALMS 1
PSALMS 14
PSALMS 21
PSALMS 30
PSALMS 45
PSALMS 50
PSALMS 87
PSALMS 108

CHAPTER 10

LIFE'S IRRITATIONS

Does life irritate you? Do people irritate you? Are you impatient with yourself and others? Are you aware of why you become irritated? *Life's Irritations* have a way of rubbing us the wrong way, especially if we do not understand how to cope, *As It Pleases God*, use the Fruits of the Spirit, behave Christlike, or fail to develop our people skills. In this chapter, you will learn how *Life's Irritations* can also rub us the right way if we strategically govern our approach, as *The Psalms Doctor* of our own life.

In the Eye of God, our attitude is everything! A good attitude can help us accomplish anything we set our minds to do. Values, beliefs, and desires really control how we behave or react to the people, places, and things around us and within us. We cannot only focus on the external elements of our people skills; we must target our people skills from the inside out. Furthermore, what we believe about ourselves becomes evident in our people skills, our approach, our perception, and our maneuverability in our daily lives.

Over the years, I have seen a great decline in the importance of having a great attitude. Actually, some people think that it's cool to be rude. Thus, in the Eye of God, a rude person expresses a lack of discipline, having a stiff neck, or dealing with dullness. Really? Yes, really!

According to the Heavenly of Heavens, rudeness is an indication of weakness, not strength. How? It is a rotten fruit. We are expected to exhibit the Fruits of the Spirit (Love, Joy, Peace, Patience, Kindness, Goodness, Faithfulness, Gentleness, and Self-Control). If we are not aligning with the Fruits of the Spirit, *As It Pleases God*, we have work to do. If not, our *Life's Irritations* are designed to become brutal with varying cycles of déjà vu with different characters.

For me, everything is based on my attitude and mindset towards it. I was taught from an early age that the right mental attitude would pave the way to my future, and it has. Now, I tell others that the right mental attitude is by far the way to go when you are on top of your game or when your game is on top of you. I firmly believe a negative attitude really slows down our effectiveness and productivity, creating poor performance and people skills.

However, some may differ with *The Psalms Doctor's* approach, especially if their pockets are padded to justify leaving a trail of rotten fruits. Still, my approach is *As It Pleases God*, not ourselves, giving us more of a reason to have a positive attitude with astounding resilience and good fruits remaining amid *Life's Irritations*.

Here is a story that is a perfect example of having a desirable scenario: Sidney has the most ideal attitude I have encountered. He is the type of person most people would love to hate or hate to love. Why? He's always in a fabulous mood; actually, he walks around daily, encouraging those who couldn't care less about being encouraged. It really seemed as if he never had a bad day.

Sidney would always walk around the office saying he was born to motivate and encourage people. Most people assumed it was fake, but I believed him. Why? Sidney represented the Fruits of the Spirit without buckling to the naysayers. Plus, his people skills were impeccable, which put me on a learning curve as well.

If someone was going through a tough time, Sidney was able to turn that person's day around without giving it a second thought. To see Sidney in action was like watching Dr. Phil. Sidney did not have a degree, but he was outstanding. His spiritual approach would put the best atheist in awe. It was so amazing to see how he could change a bad situation into a good one at the drop of a dime.

I became curious about his technique, so one day, I went up to Sidney and asked him, "How do you do it? How can you be so positive and encourage people all the time? What's your secret?" Sidney replied, "There is no secret. It's a choice. Each morning I wake up, I choose to be happy, and I ask God to give me my daily bread while allowing me to be a blessing to someone else."

Sidney also said, "Each time something bad happens, I can choose to be a victim, or I can choose to learn from it. So, I choose to learn from it and take that lesson and share it with someone else as well." "Yeah, right, it's not that simple," I replied. Then Sidney responded by saying, "Yes, it is! And that's why the simple things in life elude the best of us." He also explained that every time we hear a complaint, just point out the positive and discard the negative. He believes our life is all about the choices we make; we can choose to be and have anything.

I still had a hard time digesting the conversation I had with Sidney. Why? I thought he was feeding me a bunch of feel-good hype to woo me with his charactorial traits. Until one day, I heard he had a heart attack. I went to visit him in the hospital; I instantly began to think positively, while praying he would make it through. When I entered the room, Sidney had a smile on his face. I could not believe Sidney had something to smile about. As I began to cry, he said, "Wipe away those tears because I am going to make a full recovery, and we are going to jog a couple of miles together when I recover."

About four months after the heart attack, he was back to himself. When I asked him how he was doing, he replied, "Attitude is everything, so how about that jog?" After his ordeal, Attitude, after all, was everything.

Sidney did not wait to get a new attitude; he lived it daily. He made a full recovery because he knew beyond a shadow of a doubt that his attitude about life was his everything. It was basically through his attitude that he changed the lives of his onlookers, even me.

I must admit that when the pressure of life weighs you down, it becomes pretty challenging to have a great attitude. However, this comes with the territory of challenges when we are dealing with ultimate achievement. We must keep a great attitude, even when we are going through a tough time. The key to our breakthrough is to keep our emotions under control, not allowing negative thoughts to disrupt our peace from within, while we:

☐   Prepare ourselves daily for the next day.

- [ ] Close the chapter of what has happened in our past while understanding that it was only a lesson.
- [ ] Take advantage of the present.
- [ ] Exercise patience.
- [ ] Get ready for what is about to happen in our lives.
- [ ] Focus on where we are and where God is taking us.
- [ ] Take action to better ourselves.
- [ ] Position ourselves to be blessed.
- [ ] Move into position.
- [ ] Motivate ourselves and others.
- [ ] Use the Fruits of the Spirit.
- [ ] Respect ourselves and others.

The driving force of our passion resides in our ability to dedicate ourselves to that which is destined to challenge us. What I have definitely found in life is that anything or anyone worth having is worth working for. The dynamics of achieving success in anything or with anyone require us to persevere through our challenges to achieve a common goal. Whatever that common goal is—it is up to us, and it is our responsibility to work toward it with due diligence, *As It Pleases God.*

Do you expect the worst out of life, or do you expect the best? How often do we have an expectation about a person, place, or thing and not realize it? Our expectations are based on our experiences, biases, and self-belief. Some are fortunate enough to have all good experiences, as there will always be those who have the not so good experiences as well.

Fear of failure and the lack of self-confidence are the enemies impeding the development of our positive expectations. Suppose we fail to make the appropriate changes to counteract the effects of our negative expectations. In this case, we will soon find that it becomes challenging to move forward and embrace the opportunities that bring about positive change. When negative criticism from within the psyche dominates our thoughts, our expectations in life become very doubtful and insecure without us realizing it.

The power of our expectations is a governing factor contributing to our belief system, creating our known or unknown reality, even if we are stuck in a cycle of pretense. Our beliefs, desires, and expectations have a way of empowering us or causing us to settle for defeat.

Here is a story that fits into what I am talking about: Sissy is said to be a well-known go-getter. Whatever she wants, she puts in the hard work to attain, but she has a little problem called JEALOUSY. She had to deal with her jealous family members, who found ways to try to kill her dreams, and a little copycat sister who did not have a mind of her own.

Sissy's little sister, Margaret, never took the time to find her own dreams, aspirations, and goals in life. She found it more conducive to ride on the coattails of someone else's dreams. Although Sissy did not care about her sister's copycat syndrome, she did have a problem with how her sister treated her.

Margaret did not care who she hurt as long as she got what she wanted when she wanted it. She used Sissy to the extreme, taking her kindness for a weakness, and then talked about her behind her back as if she were the scum of the earth.

Sissy and Margaret grew up in the same home under two different sets of rules. Margaret, being the baby of the family, was nurtured to the extreme, while Sissy was neglected and treated like the scum of the earth, or better yet, an enslaved person, so to speak. Although that became Sissy's norm, she learned how to deal with her family being nice when they wanted something, and switching out on her when they did not need her. However, this form of treatment did not stop her from loving and helping others.

Sissy had to make up her mind to love herself and love others, no matter what. She also made a decision not to make others feel the pain of being neglected, nor would she allow others to kill her dream.

As years continued to roll by, Sissy continued on her pursuit of greatness, as the rest of her family envied her. She learned how to mastermind multiple ways of generating income. She came up with a system to start a lucrative business that made a fair amount of money in her spare time.

The straw that broke the camel's back was when her conniving sister used her for information to start the same business with the same system, becoming a direct competitor in the same marketplace. Her sister knew her system and how she did business, which caused her to become duplicatable. For the first time in Sissy's life, she lost her identity as being unique. Everything she did to change her approach in business, her sister emulated her and would not let up. When it came down to making money, her sister was ruthless.

After many months of prayer, God dealt with Sissy's insecurities regarding those who emulated her. From childhood, Sissy had a problem with people other than her sister copying her. If someone copied her, she would give up and do something different. As a matter of fact, Sissy felt as if she had to be the best, smartest, and greatest at everything. She did not realize that it would lead to the ultimate heartbreak of her life.

God allowed Sissy to realize that He did not allow her sister to become her competitor to surpass her. He allowed it to expose a weakness she had to deal with before He took her to the next level of living. It's amazing how Margaret betrayed her sister for the money, and Sissy learned the greatest lesson of her life before becoming a Multi-Millionaire. What was it? In the Eye of God, there was a distinct difference between emulating and duplicating when it relates to our passion and purpose.

Sissy made it her business to use *The Psalms Doctor* to better herself, as she was not going to allow the mental and emotional abuse of her past to hinder her future. For this reason, she began to pray for her daily bread as she recited the scripture in Philippians 4:13, "*I can do all things through Christ which strengthens me.*" As Sissy stepped into millionaire status, she learned how to say NO to those who choose to use her kindness as a weakness. In business, she now has over 1000 employees, while her sister Margaret is still stuck at the same level of doing business.

After all of her struggles, she wants us to learn how to trust God in all things, regardless of our past abuses, hang-ups, and setbacks.

Flaws are inevitable; we all have them. From time to time, with *Life's Irritations*, we will all feel as if nothing's working for us; however, if we allow our flaws to create undue pressure, then we will have a problem.

Luke 15:11-32 shows us how we can fall by the wayside so easily: Then He said, "*A certain man had two sons. And the younger of them said to his father, 'Father, give me the portion of goods that falls to me.' So he divided to them his livelihood. And not many days after, the younger son gathered all together, journeyed to a far country, and there wasted his possessions with prodigal living. But when he had spent all,* there arose a severe famine in that land, and he began to be in want. Then he went and joined himself to a citizen of that country, and he sent him into his fields to feed swine. And he would gladly have filled his stomach with the pods that the swine ate, and no one gave him anything. But when he came to himself, he said, 'How many of my father's hired servants have bread enough and to spare, and I perish with hunger! I will arise and go to my father, and will say to him, "Father, I have sinned against heaven and before you, and I am no longer worthy to be called your son. Make me like one of your hired servants." 'And he arose and came to his father. But when he was still a great way off, his father saw him and had compassion, and ran and fell on his neck and kissed him. And the son said to him, 'Father, I have sinned against heaven and in your sight, and am no longer worthy to be called your son.' But the father said to his servants, 'Bring out the best robe and put it on him, and put a ring on his hand and sandals on his feet. And bring the fatted calf here and kill it, and let us eat and be merry; for this my son was dead and is alive again; he was lost and is found.' And they began to be merry. Now his older son was in the field. And as he came and drew near to the house, he heard music and dancing. So he called one of the servants and asked what these things meant. And he said to him, 'Your brother has come, and because he has received him safe and sound, your father has killed the fatted calf.' But he was angry and would not go in. Therefore, his father came out and pleaded with him. So he answered and said to his father, 'Lo, these many years I have been serving you; I never transgressed your commandment at any time; and yet you never gave me a young goat, that I might make merry with my friends. But as soon as this son of yours came, who has devoured your livelihood with harlots, you killed the fatted calf for him.' And he said to him, 'Son, you are always with me, and all that I have is yours. It was right that we should make merry and be glad, for your brother was dead and is alive again, and was lost and is found.'

Life's Irritations of our flaws are created in the mind when there is codependency residing in the heart. Everything we do, say, or react to, contributes to the way in which we deal with ourselves, as well as the way in which we deal with or help others. Challenges will come, and challenges will go; therefore, we must determine what we hold on to when the challenges leave.

Some hold on to resentment, some hold on to anger, some hold on to fear, and some hold on to the ability to let go. Regardless of what we hold on to, we are held accountable for what we do with and how we react to our experiences. You are here to make a difference! It is through you that a certain amount of people can be reached, and it's your responsibility to make a positive impact on them, regardless of your set of challenges.

When dealing with *Life's Irritations*, it's okay to use our expectations to solve a problem, make a change, or empower ourselves because we are not born confident. It is a character trait that is learned and developed. Here are a few questions to ask ourselves when dissecting our *Life's Irritations*, but not limited to such:

- ☐ What is causing me to feel irritated?
- ☐ Am I overreacting to the situation?
- ☐ Have I taken the time to understand the situation entirely?
- ☐ Am I making assumptions about the situation that may not be accurate?
- ☐ Am I taking things too personally?
- ☐ Is there a deeper issue causing my irritation?
- ☐ Am I focusing too much on the negative aspects of the situation?

- ☐ Have I tried to find a solution to the problem?
- ☐ Have I communicated my concerns effectively?
- ☐ Am I holding onto past grievances that are influencing my current emotions?
- ☐ Am I taking care of myself properly, such as getting enough rest and exercise?
- ☐ Am I allowing others to influence my emotions too much?
- ☐ Am I practicing gratitude and focusing on the positive aspects of my life?
- ☐ Am I placing too much importance on things that don't truly matter?
- ☐ Am I trying to control things that are outside of my control?
- ☐ Am I setting unrealistic expectations for myself or others?
- ☐ Am I taking responsibility for my own emotions and reactions?
- ☐ Have I considered seeking outside help or support?
- ☐ Am I forgiving myself and others for mistakes and shortcomings?
- ☐ Am I approaching the situation with an open and curious mindset rather than a closed and rigid one?

Regardless of where we are with our *Life's Irritations*, whatever we have learned in the past can be unlearned, relearned, or regrafted, especially if we are willing to change our expectations and ask the right questions. If we work through our weaknesses to free ourselves, *As It Pleases God*, use the Fruits of the Spirit, and behave Christlike, we will develop impeccable people skills, guaranteed! As *The Psalms Doctor*, I am living proof!

PRAYER

Father, my God, in the Name of Jesus, I take authority over all *Life's Irritations*. I come to You today with a heavy heart, weighed down by the many irritations and frustrations of life. I know that these are small in the grand scheme of things, but they can sometimes feel overwhelming. Lord, please help me to find the strength and patience to deal with my challenges like a champion. Help me to see the bigger picture and to remember that everything happens for a reason, even if I may not understand it at the time.

My Father, grant me the peacefulness to accept the things I cannot change with an understanding, *As It Pleases You*. More importantly, with the unction of the Holy Spirit, please give me the courage to change and ask the right questions to query myself to unveil my hidden truths or lies. With Your love and guidance, I am moving forward in the Spirit of Excellence with the wisdom and integrity to know what to do, when to do it, why to do it, where to do it, and with whom. In Jesus' Name. Amen.

SCRIPTURE READING:

PSALMS 62
PSALMS 76
PSALMS 95
PSALMS 105

CHAPTER 11

TRUE LIVING

Are you living your truth? Is your truth living or lying to you? Are you becoming barricaded by truth and lies? Is the decimation of True Living becoming a fantasy? According to the Heavenly of Heavens, True Living is on the table, *As It Pleases God* or to please ourselves. Unfortunately, lukewarm living is not an option in the Eye of God.

Massive exposure is on the horizon; we must cultivate our authenticity, *As It Pleases God*, or the wolves in sheep's clothing will feast at our table. What does this mean? We cannot save everyone, but it's our responsibility to do our part in making a true difference. Throughout my journey in life, I have found that communication is one of our most invaluable commodities. If we have a desire to be understood, we must first understand through effective listening. When we do not listen, we will find we tend to miss out on the essence of what true living is all about.

This story really moved me: While in the heart of beautiful downtown Orlando, a man sat down next to a woman on a bench near the swan rides at Lake Eola Park. "That's my daughter over there," he said, pointing to a cute little redhead girl who was mesmerized by the beautiful swans that were walking around freely without a care in the world. "She's a cutie pie, and that's my son on the swan boat ride," the woman said. Then, looking at her watch, she called to her son. "It's time to go, Blake." He pleaded, "Just one more ride, Mom. Please...Just one more ride, please." The woman nodded, and Blake continued another 30-minute ride. When the ride ended, she said, "Let's go, Blake...We need to leave; we have already spent $36.00 on this Swan ride."

Again, Blake pleaded, "One more time, Mom. Just one more." The woman politely smiled and said, "Okay, we only have enough money for one more ride." The man next to her said, "My, you do not see too many mothers as patient as you are." The woman smiled and then said, "I waited 20 years for God to bless me with a son; therefore, the time his dad and I spend with him is well worth understanding his need to have fun. My goal is to listen and understand his wants, needs, and desires, so if Blake needs 30 more minutes to ride on the Swan, that means I have 30 more minutes to understand he is worth the time I spend waiting on him."

This woman took the time to digest *The Psalms Doctor* in order to exercise patience and the value of spending quality time with her son.

When we are at the crossroads of survival, the thoughts we think determine the real essence of who we are, what we will become, what or whom we attract, and which direction we take. One of the biggest issues we all face is figuring out what to do with our lives.

Nevertheless, in the figuring process, we often get our insurance policies together, preparing for death, forgetting about preparing to live. Living our lives to the fullest is often overlooked because we become so busy going from here to there, not realizing there is more to life than our present situation.

I ran across this story several years ago; please allow me to share. One day, a farmer's donkey fell into a well. The helpless donkey cried pitifully for hours as the little old farmer tried to figure out what he was going to do. Finally, he decided the animal was old; he had already gotten the use out of him, and the well needed to be covered up anyway.

He believed it just was not worth it to rescue the donkey from the well. So he decided he would invite all of his neighbors over to help him cover up the poor old donkey. They all grabbed a shovel and began to scoop dirt into the well. When the donkey realized his master had given up on him, he cried.

The wailing of a donkey should pierce the heart of anyone, but no one cared; they kept throwing dirt on him as if his life meant nothing. He could not believe he had faithfully served his master for so many years, and now that he was in a predicament, his master had given up on him without a fight. Then, to the amazement of everyone, he stopped crying.

He decided to do something about his situation. The more they piled dirt on him, the more he used it as a stepping stone to get out of his predicament. As the farmer and his friends kept shoveling dirt, they finally looked down and saw that the donkey was not settling for defeat. Every time they shoveled dirt on the donkey, he would shake it off and take another step up.

The farmer and his friends could not believe the donkey was smart enough to step up out of his situation. Soon enough, the donkey stepped right over the edge and walked off, leaving his old master behind, refusing to look back.

Our enemies will become our footstool of greatness if we allow them to play their role in our lives. This mindset will enable us to become a cornerstone, especially if we do not become bitter about the circumstances or situations that are presented to us. It's through our enemies that we will find what *True Living* is all about.

According to the Heavenly of Heavens, negative thoughts and emotions inhibit our ability to grab the source of wisdom needed to make all of our enemies become the footstool that's propelling us to the next level. In the Eye of God, we must allow our enemies to make us better, not bitter. Why? When we are bitter, we actually prevent wisdom from attaching itself to us. As a matter of fact, bitterness opens the door to jealousy, envy, pride, greed, coveting, and competitiveness to further break down the emotional or mental bonds. What does this mean? Simply put, it breaks down relationships.

True Living is not what people think or say about you that matters; it's what you are saying about yourself that really makes the difference. So what...If people throw dirt at you or on you. Just step up to the next level with your head up high as you learn how to develop the voice within, the counselor of your higher self. Here are a few questions to elevate your mind when dirt is thrown on you, but not limited to such:

- ☐ What does it mean to live your truth?
- ☐ How can you identify your personal truth?
- ☐ What are some common barriers to living your truth?
- ☐ How can you overcome those barriers?
- ☐ What role does authenticity play in living your truth?
- ☐ How can you cultivate authenticity in your life?
- ☐ What is the connection between living your truth and happiness?

- [ ] What are some examples of people who have successfully lived their truth?
- [ ] How can you balance living your truth with meeting the expectations of others?
- [ ] What are some ways you can stay true to yourself while still being open to growth and change?
- [ ] What are some common misconceptions about living your truth?
- [ ] How can you navigate difficult conversations or situations while still staying true to yourself?
- [ ] What are some strategies for coping with the fear or discomfort that can come with living your truth?
- [ ] How can you support others in living their truth?
- [ ] What role does vulnerability play in living your truth?
- [ ] How can you practice self-compassion in the process of living your truth?
- [ ] What is the connection between living your truth and living a lie?
- [ ] How can you integrate your personal truth into your daily lives?
- [ ] What are some practices or habits that can help you stay true to yourself?
- [ ] How can you continue to grow and evolve while remaining authentic to your truth?

God has given you the Holy Spirit as your counselor to help you answer these questions. Why the questions? They are healing to the human psyche. Allow Him to work for you and through you to accomplish your goals and aspirations in life, *As It Pleases God*. According to *The Psalms Doctor*, a PSALM a day will keep the tricks of the enemy at bay!

PRAYER

Father, my God, which art in Heaven, I come before You with a humble heart and a sincere desire to be authentic in all I do, say, and become. Father, in *True Living*, You know me better than I know myself, and You love me unconditionally. Help me to be honest with myself and with others, to speak the truth in love, and to act with integrity and compassion. Forgive me for the times when I have been false, hypocritical, or insincere. Renew my mind and transform my heart, so I may reflect Your image and glorify Your name.

Lord, I also come to You in prayer for dealing with people who throw dirt on me. You know how hard it is to face those who slander, gossip, or lie about me. You know the pain and anger that I feel in my heart. You also know the temptation to retaliate or to harbor bitterness. Lord, I ask You to help me overcome these negative emotions and to respond with grace, kindness, pristineness, and wisdom.

My God, You are the judge of all, and You will vindicate the righteous and expose the wicked, *As It Pleases You*. Help me to trust in Your promises and to follow Your commands. Help me to love my enemies and to pray for those who persecute me. Please allow me to become a peacemaker and a bridge-builder, not a troublemaker or a divider.

Lord, I thank You for Your presence, forgiveness, mercy, grace, and strength with *The Psalms Doctor*. In Jesus' name, Amen.

Dr. Y. Bur

SCRIPTURE READING:

PSALMS 23
PSALMS 25
PSALMS 40
PSALMS 65
PSALMS 66

THE PSALMS DOCTOR NEEDS' LIST

Purpose	Psalm
Abundance	23
Aligning Your Thoughts	71
Anger	73
Anointing Home	108
Answers From God	141
Anxiety	31
Anxiety	12
Anxiety	13
Appreciation For Blessings	30
Assistance From God Daily	132
Assuming Responsibility	82
Assurance In Time Of Need	99
Attacks	28
Attitude Of Gratitude	66
Attract Good Business	8
Attract Greatness	84
Awareness	95
Bad Habits	69
Bad Influences	68
Bad Memories	105
Balance	52
Battle	20
Be Anxious For Nothing	55
Bearing A Heavy Load	145
Bedtime Prayer	4
Betrayal	41
Blessed Business	8
Blessed Hands	113

Escape	11
Escape Wicked Plots	101
Evil Eye Protection	36
Evil Suppression	109
Failure	117
Fairness	149
Faith	5
Faith	19
Faith	81
Falsely Accused	94
Favor	5
Favor	20
Favor	123
Favor For Finances	5
Favor On High	113
Favor With Customers	8
Favorable Verdict	20
Fear	3
Fear	32
Fear Of The Unknown	33
Fight For What's Yours	11
Fighting A Battle	83
Fighting Discouragement	142
Fighting Discouragement	63
Financial Help	72
Find Yourself	44
Flourish	132
Flourish	115
Forgiveness	85
Forgiveness	15
Forgiveness	25

Forgiveness	75
Forgiveness	103
Forgiveness	119
Friendliness	67
Friendliness	133
Frustrated	40
Frustrated With Life	40
Fulfillment	111
Future Plans	84
Gain Power	130
Gateway To A Higher Self	23
Get Rid Of Pride	131
Giving Thanks	65
Good Energy	123
Good Fortune	74
Good Life	16
Good Ventures	112
Gossip	12
Grace	36
Grace	103
Gratefulness	66
Gratefulness	65
Gratefulness	150
Gratefulness For Life	116
Gratitude	66
Great Aspirations In Life	135
Great Attitude	116
Growth	5
Growth	14
Guidance	1
Guidance	50

Kind Heart	27
Kindness	123
Learning Good Habits	119
Led To A New Place In God	61
Liberation	71
Lies	12
Loneliness	23
Loneliness	31
Loneliness	148
Longsuffering	6
Longsuffering	52
Love	19
Love	53
Love	111
Lovers	88
Loving Environment	33
Lucky	76
Lucky Hand	76
Make Peace	28
Meekness	110
Meekness	131
Mental Affirmations	54
Mental Exhaustion	31
Mental Stability	125
Mercy	4
Mercy	6
Mercy	20
Mercy	23
Mercy	136
Mercy From God	51
Mercy In Court	99

Temptation	56
Tension	31
Tension Relief	2
Thanksgiving	66
Thanksgiving	30
Thanksgiving	90
Time Of Need	24
Time Of Trouble	20
Tranquility	37
Trials & Tribulations	69
Triumph Over Enemies	11
Trouble	27
Trust	16
Trusting God	106
Trusting God	139
Truth Exposed	35
Unblock Success	95
Unity	97
Universal Provision	81
Unjust Happenings	43
Victory	132
Victory	76
Victory In A Battle	37
Victory In Court Case	35
Wavering Faith	96
When Overwhelmed With Issues	118
Wisdom	23

PLEASE SEND **THE PSALMS DOCTOR** PRAYERS, TESTIMONIES, DONATIONS, OR ORDERS TO:

Dr. Y. Bur
R.O.A.R. Publishing Group
581 N. Park Ave. Ste. #725
Apopka, FL 32704
ROAR-58-2316
762-758-2316

Email:
Dr.YBur@gmail.com

Order Books Online At:
www. *DrYBur*.com

Please Donate

Please DONATE to this *Missionable Movement of God* as a GIVE-BACK to the Kingdom. Thanks for your support. Many Blessings.

Donation QR Code

www.ingramcontent.com/pod-product-compliance
Lightning Source LLC
Chambersburg PA
CBHW070813100426
42742CB00012B/2343